Hannah

Regina

Britain's Quaker Queen

*"All the world is queer save thee and
me, and even thou art a little queer."*

Robert Owen (attrib).

Michael Kreps

Michael Kreps has also written:

To the Devil with Opera!

First Published 2002
Second (revised) Edition 2003

Cardinal Press
9 Foreland Court
London NW4 1LG

© Michael Kreps

ISBN: 0 9533505 7

A CIP record for this book is available from the British Library.

Typeset in Eurostar 12 pt.

For

Simon & Paula

and for

Jake & Abigail

With sincere thanks and appreciation to
Mrs Clare Hopkins, Archivist at Trinity College, Oxford,
for her invaluable help on Dr James Wilmot.

And to my Editor, Susan Dixon, for clarifying the chaos,
confusion and clutter in the original manuscript submitted to
her.

Portrait of a Lady

Joshua Reynolds

Preface To The 2nd Edition

The original edition of this book has sold so encouragingly well that I have taken the opportunity to revise and rework certain chapters and to introduce additional material not previously available. For instance, the DNA testing of the Mackelcans of America, and of the Rex family of South Africa; the result of the Privy Council's inquiry into the Duke of Cumberland's marriage to Anne Horton; and certain detail material such as the identification of the cleric who officiated at King George and Queen Charlotte's re-marriage in 1765 (who interestingly was a future Archbishop of Canterbury), This revised edition should as a result be both a clearer and a still more convincing exposition of the argument that King George III, whilst Prince of Wales, did indeed marry Hannah Lightfoot, his 'fair Quaker', on 17th April 1759, and that therefore his later marriage, on 8th September 1761 to Princess Charlotte of Mecklenburg-Strelitz, was not a valid marriage (which was why they went through that second ceremony four years later).

This story, like the 18th century in which it is set, is full of fascinating Characters. The scoundrelly 'Dr' Alexander Keith; Elizabeth Chudleigh, Duchess of Kingston, who has been described as one of the greatest adventuresses of her time; her legal husband, who only fleetingly appears in these pages, Vice-Admiral the Earl of Bristol who was not merely a great fighting sailor in the tradition of the times but also, and equally traditionally, had women in every part of the world that he visited. There is Anne Horton's brother Colonel Luttrell, who only by lies and bribery narrowly escaped conviction for debauching a young girl, who was a brutal but brilliant and controversial soldier, and who once declined a challenge to a duel from his own father on the grounds that "(he) is not a gentleman", yet is said to have forced the ungentlemanly Duke of Cumberland to marry his sister by threatening him with a duel; or the quiet but influential cleric-cum-courtier Dr James Wilmot, who started the 'Who was Shakespeare?' controversy that continues today. We have his very talented granddaughter Mrs Olive Wilmot Serres, whose determination to obtain her rights was ultimately responsible for exposing the whole Lightfoot affair; and there was the mysterious General Mackelcan who, without any of the advantages of birth, money, or even it must be said any outstanding military talent, nevertheless rose like a rocket through the ranks of the army to become a full General at the astonishingly early age of 37. And last, but by no means least there were the Royal Hanovers whose Head, King George III, was so convinced of his own wisdom over that of such great Statesmen as William Pitt, Earl of Chatham, that he went to war and lost the American Colonies. And within this starry cast was the young Quaker woman Hannah Lightfoot, the almost invisible central character about whom the whole plot revolves, a young woman who was so modest and retiring that she wouldn't even demand recognition as King George's rightful Queen.

MK

Contents

Introduction

Hannah Lightfoot—an imaginary portrait

On 12ᵗʰ April 1759, whilst he was still Prince of Wales, King George III secretly, at Kew Chapel, married his mistress of some five years standing, a Quaker named Hannah Lightfoot. Six weeks later, on 27ᵗʰ May, he confirmed that commitment with a second ceremony at their Peckham residence, this marriage, like the earlier one at Kew, being conducted by the Reverend Dr. James Wilmot. Just eighteen months later, on 25ᵗʰ October 1760 his grandfather King George II died and he became King George III. Within his first year as Sovereign, on the 8ᵗʰ September 1761, with Hannah Lightfoot, the mother of his children being still married to him, still unacknowledged but nevertheless now his Queen, he went through another but this time very public ceremony of marriage, to Charlotte Sophia of Mecklenburgh-Strelitz, a Protestant princess who was presented to the Country as Queen Charlotte. The unacknowledged Queen Hannah made no public protest.

The King's brother, Henry Frederick Duke of Cumberland, had a very similar marital history. For on 4th March 1767 he quietly married Miss Olive Wilmot, who was Dr. James Wilmot's daughter. On 2nd October 1771, ten years all but a few days after his eldest brother's second marriage, and with his wife Olive three months pregnant with their child, he too, like his brother, married again. His new bride was Mrs Anne Horton, who became his official Duchess just as Charlotte had become his brother's official Queen.

Almost one hundred years later, in June 1866 a trial took place in an Appeal Court which, under the pretext of examining certain claims of Olive Wilmot's granddaughter, was actually used as a pseudo-judicial procedure intended to dispose finally of all the rumours, which had continued to circulate for over 100 years, concerning George III's marriage to Hannah Lightfoot. The evidence of the first marriages of the King and his brother Cumberland had become so entangled that no investigation of the one could be carried out without exposing the other; and the claims of Olive Wilmot's granddaughter had everything to do with the matter of the Duke of Cumberland's marriage to Olive Wilmot. For this reason this 1866 trial, which officially investigated Olive Wilmot's granddaughter's claims concerning her descent from the Duke of Cumberland, proved to be a travesty. It was no more than a quasi-legal procedure within one of England's senior courts to cover up, by denial, his marriage to her grandmother (and thus also that of King George to Hannah Lightfoot) and pretend it never happened. Yet although the trial succeeded in one objective of finally silencing Olive Wilmot's granddaughter, it only succeeded in stimulating, not killing off, the interest in George III's clandestine marriage to Hannah Lightfoot. The rumours did *not* die as the Judges had intended although, like Rip van Winkle, certain aspects were put to sleep for a hundred years. This study sets out to put the record straight concerning George and Hannah, and indeed the Duke of Cumberland and his own marital affairs.

The Duke's first wife Olive Wilmot and her unborn child were put away. In January 1820 George III. died; Olive Wilmot herself had long been dead. But her daughter, also called Olive, who had been brought up by Dr Wilmot's brother Robert and his wife and thus believed Dr Wilmot to be her uncle, had by now learned the secret of her birth and began in earnest a campaign for recognition as the Duke of Cumberland's daughter, to be recognised therefore as a member of the Royal Family, and to receive the financial benefits which had been provided by the King for his brother's then unborn daughter (ie herself). This campaign, which was unsuccessful during her lifetime, reached its culmination many years after her death in the 1866 trial brought about by *her* daughter Mrs Lavinia Ryves, a trial in which the Judges quite literally 'rubbished' her claims in the face of convincing evidence of their truth. This was because the documentation relating to Mrs Ryves' (and her late mother's) claims demonstrated that the Duke of Cumberland had indeed married Miss Olive Wilmot, *and in turn* that showed that the late King George III had in fact married Hannah Lightfoot. Inevitably such a proof not merely of the King's but of a double Royal bigamy would expose a major constitutional problem concerning the Royal Succession following George's death, so to avoid Parliament and the Country having to face this problem the Court followed a deliberate plan to show that these earlier legitimate marriages of both the King and his brother never happened, and that therefore the two later marriages, to Queen Charlotte and to Mrs Horton, were legitimate. The consequences of the ten-year reign of an illegitimate sovereign (George IV), and the matter of his successors were never to be challenged, and Olive Wilmot's granddaughter (not to mention her late daughter) and descendants were forever deprived of certain of their constitutional rights and inheritance.

This study denies the outcome of the 1866 trial. It sets out and examines the evidence that King George had properly and legitimately married Hannah Lightfoot before he married Queen Charlotte; that Hannah was still living and married to him at the time of this second marriage and at the time of the birth of his two eldest sons by Queen Charlotte; and, therefore, that the Succession of George IV in 1820 was invalid. It is also demonstrated that the Duke of Cumberland had properly married Olive Wilmot and therefore that his subsequent marriage to Anne Horton was bigamous. These proofs, which were not available for a hundred years after the 1866 trial, can now be seen by anyone who wants to look at them, in the Public Records Office at Kew.

The story begins with George, the young Prince of Wales's infatuation as a teenager with a young woman, Hannah Lightfoot, who has become known to history as 'the fair quaker'. She was an obscure Quaker girl of the early eighteenth century, so obscure that even now little is known about her, yet she has continued to intrigue people down the centuries that have followed her appearance as the 'secret' mistress of George, Prince of Wales. She seems only to have done one thing in her entire life that was of any interest, but that single act—her marriage to the Heir to the Throne—is the source of all the interest in her. This marriage has been the subject of speculation and discussion ever since it was 'supposed' to have taken place; 'supposed' because it was never satisfactorily proved to have occurred. Although London and the Royal Court knew about 'Mistress' Hannah, and it was rumoured that she was now 'Queen' Hannah, it was just that, rumour. There was no proof, and since Hannah herself was too meek and self-effacing to do anything about it, no-one else took any radical steps to protest about the King's marriage to Queen Charlotte. After all, the union to Hannah Lightfoot, even if it were true, would have been widely regarded as totally unsuitable so perhaps it was better to ignore it, or better still to assume that it hadn't happened and that she was still just his mistress. For by invalidating George's later marriage to Queen Charlotte, it would follow that the legitimacy of all successive monarchs was also brought into question. But who was his rightful Queen? Hannah Lightfoot? Or Princess Charlotte?

Charlotte herself was sufficiently concerned about the persistent rumours and stories concerning the Lightfoot marriage that she is supposed to have insisted on going through a second marriage ceremony. This was said to have been carried out under cover of a mid-summer entertainment at Kew Palace. Even so, and assuming it happened, this second ceremony could have been valid only if there were definite knowledge that Hannah had died, and to this day there is no absolute information about *when,* or even where she died.

The stories about this marriage of Hannah Lightfoot to the Prince of Wales, which took root around the time that he married Princess Charlotte, have never gone away. Even forty years after the event they were firmly believed as far away as South Africa, where one of Hannah's reputed sons was sent. They are true. King George did marry Hannah before he married Princess Charlotte, and since Hannah was still living when he ascended the throne, she was his rightful Queen. And the first direct consequence of this is that Charlotte's eldest son George (later King George IV) was not, in fact, entitled to be king because he was, as he himself is supposed to have taunted his parents, their bastard son. The proof, held in the Public Records Office at Kew, is analysed here.

It ought to be a very straightforward matter these days to determine whether or not George, whilst Prince of Wales, married Hannah Lightfoot. The primary evidence consists of various documents held in the Public Records Office directly attesting to the marriage, including *two* wedding certificates each complete with witness signatures of significant people of the day. There is also Hannah's Will in which she, signing herself 'Hannah Regina', refers to 'my Husband His Majesty King George III'. In the trial of June 1866, in a sweeping condemnation of these and all the other documents presented at the same time, they were roundly declared by the Judges to be forgeries, *against firm evidence* from the leading handwriting expert of the day and many others, that they were genuine. The Special Jury agreed with the Judges. These certificates, together with all the other documents were then impounded and whilst they can now be seen at the Public Records Office, it is still a problem to determine their authenticity. A straightforward comparison of signatures to confirm (or not) the opinions of the handwriting expert and others of 150 years ago is no longer sufficient. Today's forensic experts also want, after this lapse of time, to test the age both of the papers and the inks to ensure that these are themselves some 250 years old (most of the documents have dates around the mid-eighteenth century). This 'age' test also would be particularly valuable in determining whether the papers are originals or, as the Judges claimed, later substitutes; clearly without all of these tests there can be no authoritative forensic review of the 1866 trial outcome. However the Public Records Office will not allow any procedures that might involve destructive testing or in any way damage the integrity of the documents in their care, so this relatively straightforward approach to resolving the question is not available. This study therefore takes an alternative route to obtaining an answer which involves a wide trawl through that remarkably similar situation, the first marriage of the King's youngest brother Henry, Duke of Cumberland, the evidence for which became so entangled with that for George's marriage to Hannah Lightfoot.

It is then necessary to separate fact from fiction concerning the various stories told by Mrs Olive Wilmot Serres, Cumberland's only child of his marriage to Olive Wilmot (there were no children from his later marriage to Anne Horton) about her origins. She originally produced all these documents as part of her efforts to establish herself as the Duke's daughter, and then surrounded them with so many different and inconsistent stories that she almost destroyed both their credibility and her own. This study therefore is at times less concerned with Hannah Lightfoot and King George, much more with the consequences of the King's use of the Oxford cleric the Rev. Dr James Wilmot, Dr Wilmot's use of his brother Robert and his sister Mrs Olive Payne, and the Royals' relationships with Dr Wilmot and his family.

Hannah Lightfoot
(aka Mrs Axford)

Dr Alexander Keith

Little is known about Hannah Lightfoot or her background, although her family tree has been established. She was the daughter of Matthew Lightfoot, a shoemaker from Yorkshire and his wife Mary (née Wheeler), a Quaker couple who lived in Wapping, East London, where Hannah was born on 12th October 1730. Her father died in 1732 and about three years later Hannah and her mother — there had been a boy, John, born in the year of his father's death but he lived only a year — moved to St. James' Market, London (now re-developed and incorporated into the Piccadilly end of Regent Street in modern London) to live with her uncle, Mary's bachelor brother Henry Wheeler, also a Quaker. Henry soon afterwards further expanded his household with the acquisition of a wife, and then four children. His drapery shop and business was profitable enough for him to keep not only this large family but also, later on, a maid (not a Quaker girl) of about Hannah's age with whom Hannah became good friends and who seems to have had a small part in the Hannah Lightfoot story. For even when, in due course, the maid married and left to take up a position within the household where her husband was employed, this friendship continued. It was probably through this young woman, whose name is thought to be Anne Tayler, that Hannah initially gained whatever worldly knowledge she may have acquired outside of her life in St. James' Market and the Society of Friends.

Although she was "considered one of the beautiful women of her time, and rather disposed to *embonpoint*", there is nothing available today to suggest that Hannah Lightfoot had any special beauty or a particularly sparkling personality. She was one of the relatively few young women of her time to have escaped the ravages of the smallpox disease that was around and perhaps for that reason has been variously described as 'the beautiful quakeress', and 'the fair quaker' by the many people who, particularly over the years following the 1866 trial, wrote letters about her to the correspondence columns of journals. A surviving portrait of her does not suggest any special physical attractions, possibly because it would have been painted when she was older, about thirty, and at a time of unhappiness in her life, ie when she could perhaps sense that her great romance was coming to an end as the King's affections and interests were becoming engaged elsewhere.

She appears to have been a quite unsophisticated person; just a nice young woman who was so bowled over by the youthful ardour (and rank) of her princely suitor that she could abandon a lifetime's strict religious upbringing. At the age of twenty-three she consented to a marriage that she intended *immediately* to walk away from. She willingly co-operated, before this marriage could be consummated, in an act that was totally in contradiction of her entire upbringing and way of life, ie in her own dramatic abduction and elopement in order to go and live with her fifteen-year old Royal admirer. She would never again see any member of her family or circle of friends, and she would spend virtually the rest of her life hidden away in grand houses waiting for visits from her lover whenever his State affairs permitted him to get away to her. For her, this could not have been infatuation; this must have been *Love*, an emotion, a passion which whilst it provided her Prince and herself with three children, would ultimately lead to her being effectively abandoned by him. She died at an unknown age, and lies buried in an unknown grave in an unknown location (albeit subject to stories about a grave in an Islington church with someone else's name on the headstone).

It all began, so legend has it, when the young Prince George saw a lovely girl sitting in the window of her uncle's shop in St James's, watching the Royal procession of sedan chairs, chairmen, carriages, footmen and so on of which he was part, on their way to the theatre in Drury Lane. He engineered several opportunities to observe this attractive young woman (she was some eight years older than him), almost certainly using the assistance of Miss Elizabeth Chudleigh, one of his mother's Maids of Honour.

Even though he had a strongly religious turn of mind and a dislike of his family's morality, George was nevertheless both a Hanover and a teenager and had inherited the family's active hormones. It wasn't long, therefore, before he was involved in secret rendezvous' with Hannah, initially at private rooms in the Haymarket, ably assisted by the experienced Miss Chudleigh. Only ten years older than Hannah, yet light years older in the ways of the world, her skill in identifying and making use of the services of the friendly ex-maid and others enabled her to involve Hannah's initial interest. It was of course not possible, even for someone as sophisticated in these matters as Miss Chudleigh, to ensure total secrecy about the Prince of Wales's affair; to the contrary, for it is thought that for her own advantage she informed George's mother Princess Augusta, of the developing relationship. With alarm spreading both through the Court and within the devoutly Quaker Wheeler household once it was confirmed, arrangements were made to end it, and swiftly. A young acquaintance of Hannah's, a grocer's shop assistant named Isaac Axford, was set up to marry her. He knew and liked her but a handsome bribe paid from Court sources no doubt helped his ardour. It was agreed all round that haste was important; so much so that, instead of waiting for the normal preliminaries to take place that would enable the marriage ceremony to be performed at the Society of Friends Meeting House, which was the obvious place for a wedding between two Quakers living in London, it took place on 11th December 1753 at Keith's Wedding Chapel in Curzon Street, Mayfair. This was the best known of a number of similarly dubious 'marriage mills' where, for a fee, a marriage could be immediately and legitimately contracted without delays, without any inconvenient publicity such as banns, without any enquiries being made, and even without a licence.

The Rev. Dr Alexander Keith was quite a character. He has been described as a man of some academic distinction, having an MA and a DD from Oxford. Probably this 'distinction' was his own description, just as his degrees appear to have been his own invention, since there are no records of him ever having attended Oxford (or Cambridge) University, let alone being awarded a DD. He is thought to have started his marriage business when he was in the Fleet debtors prison and at a time when the matrimonial laws of the country were just a disgraceful mess. There were many women debtors in the prison and a married woman was not then liable for her own debts: it was her husband who was. So, for a consideration Keith, and many other Ministers of the Church operating around the Fleet in particular, found men who were prepared to marry them, and then for a fee carried out the ceremony. These men might be other inmates with no hope of paying off their own debts, so adding those of an unknown woman, perhaps in exchange for sex and a meaningless promise that once released she would work to pay off his debt, was something the inmate could be readily persuaded of by such a smart operator as 'Dr' Keith. Others might be the drunken clients of prostitutes brought to the prison for Keith and other operators to unite with them, thereby providing the women with complete immunity from any present or future debt problem. One man, tried for bigamy, denied all knowledge of the woman supposed to be his bigamous wife; after a drunken evening he'd woken up to find himself in bed with her; "I'm your wife my dear, we were married last night at the Fleet." These marriages procedures were legal. Not that it mattered much, for there was virtually no investigation into the possibility of them being bigamous marriages, or whether the names of the parties were genuine, or even if they were man and woman, and 'Dr' Keith no doubt carried out his fair share of these. After all if no one else was asking questions there was no reason why he should. Evidence to Parliament stated that in the four-month period between October 1704 and February 1705 almost 3,000 unlicensed marriages were performed in the Fleet alone, never mind elsewhere. Keith's business prospered, he paid off his debts and, around 1730, once outside, used his money to buy some land in the village of May Fair just outside London, built a small chapel on it and advertised his services. In *The Daily Post* of 20th July 1744, for instance, one can read that

...to prevent mistakes, the little new chapel in May Fair, near Hyde Park Corner, is in the corner-house opposite to the city side of the Great Chapel and within yards of it. The minister and clerk live in the same corner-house where the little chapel is: and the licence on the common stamp, minister and clerk's fees, together with the certificate amount to one guinea as heretofore, and at any hour till four in the afternoon. And that it may be better known there is a porch at the door like a country church porch.

The way to the chapel is through Piccadilly by the end of St. James's Street, down Clarges Street, and turn to the left hand.

His clientele there varied from the aristocratic, to the merely shady, or those simply in a hurry to wed; there was the dissipated Duke of Hamilton (former fiancé of Elizabeth Chudleigh) who, in 1752 married there Elizabeth, the younger of the famously beautiful Gunning sisters who had by then displaced Miss Chudleigh as the finest beauty at Court; according to Horace Walpole there was the 'young fellow' who chased a girl round Hyde Park and then to her home late at night, and besieged her there until, two to three days later she surrendered and agreed to go with him immediately (at four in the morning) to Keith's. He however refused to get up at that hour 'not even to marry the King' and referred them to a more accommodating parson who presumably had a greater need of the money. Another Duke who took advantage of Keith's services was the Duke of Chandos who, staying at an Inn on his way to London saw an Ostler there abusing his wife, a chambermaid at the Inn, whom he was leading about with a halter round her neck; appalled at such treatment as much as he was taken with her beauty, the Duke purchased (!) the woman from the Ostler, took her back with him, made her his mistress and, learning a few years later that her husband had died, married her on Xmas day at Keith's Chapel, thus making her his Duchess.

Keith became so famous, constructing according to Walpole 'a very bishopric of revenue' that after a few years the Church could no longer ignore him. He was denounced by Dr Trebeck, the Rector at the adjoining parish of St. George's, Hanover Square. At the inquiry in 1742, Keith claimed to have been admitted to the priesthood by the Bishop of Norwich on recommendation from the Bishop of London (oddly, he didn't mention his DD). The inquiry found against him and in October of that year he was excommunicated for simony. Instead of ending his career however the excommunication turned out to be quite a help to him, for if your problems were such that you were thinking of getting 'Dr' Keith to marry you, the Church had just made the decision a lot easier: if you didn't want the marriage to be binding you only had to 'discover' later on that he had been excommunicated. But, angered by the Church's action, he decided that if they could excommunicate him, an accredited priest, he could excommunicate them and so, to considerable acclaim from his supporters (and there were many) he 'excommunicated' the Bishop of London Dr Edmund Gibson, Dr Trebeck, and Dr Andrews the Judge of the Court concerned in the proceedings against him. Then, to show his contempt for those proceedings, he followed that with a mass marrying of some sixty couples. The Church retaliated by accusing him of blasphemy and succeeded in having him sent back, in April 1743, to prison for six years. From there he continued to run his marriage business, both at Mayfair and in prison, via curate assistants.

Yet in spite of his strictly commercial attitude to other peoples' marriages it appeared that he may have had a more conventional and caring view concerning his own. His wife died while he was in prison and he was able to insist that her body be embalmed until his release when he could bury her himself. During this period four of his children also died. The body of one of these he arranged in 1748 to be transported on a bier to St. Paul's church in Covent Garden with notices on the bier concerning his complaints at his treatment; the men in charge were instructed to make frequent stops in order to allow people to read these notices.

In 1753, however, the Clandestine Marriages Act *(The Act for the Better Preventing of Clandestine Marriages)* was passed, which finally ended his operations. It was possibly the clause, which promised that anyone solemnising a marriage outside of the provisions of the Act

...shall be transported to some of his Majesty's plantations in America for the space of fourteen years according to the laws in force for the transportation of felons...

that finally convinced 'Dr' Keith that he couldn't continue. In 1753 he published a pamphlet entitled *Observations on the Act for Preventing Clandestine Marriages*, which carried a picture of himself entitled 'The Rev. Mr Keith DD'. Interestingly, this Act, which applied only to England and

Wales, specifically excluded from its embrace the Royal Family, Quakers and Jews. It might almost have been designed by and on behalf of Prince George to protect his future clandestine marriage to Hannah Lightfoot, (and thirty two years later that of his eldest son's, the future George IV, marriage to Mrs FitzHerbert). Keith, eventually having exhausted his resources, was sent back to prison, where he died in December 1758.

Back in December 1753 Mrs Hannah Axford, née Lightfoot, stepped outside Keith's Chapel into a waiting coach (reputedly with Miss Chudleigh inside it as her escort—this lady was adept at being on both sides of an affair) and was driven off at speed. Unsuccessfully pursued by her bridegroom, she was never seen again by her family or friends, despite searches by her husband and by the Society of Friends. After three years of fruitless searches, the Friends then expelled her from their Society. There is a story that around the time of the expulsion Axford, still searching for his wife, even appealed in St James's Park, on his knees, directly to the Prince of Wales to return her. If true this story at least makes the point that London was aware of Prince George's liaison with Hannah Lightfoot.

The official reason given by the Quakers for Hannah's expulsion was stated to be her marriage to 'one not of our Society'. This expulsion for 'marrying out' was always one of the lesser Lightfoot mysteries for she hadn't (yet) married George and although there was no absolute proof that Isaac Axford was a Quaker, it always seemed unlikely that such devout people as Henry Wheeler and his sister Mary Lightfoot would countenance the marriage of Hannah to anyone other than a Quaker, even in the dire circumstances of her Royal liaison. Recent research, however, has established that the Axfords were, in fact, a Baptist family. The reason given by the Friends for her expulsion was thus technically correct, but since many other Quakers were known to have married out without being expelled, it was almost certainly not the real reason. More likely the Friends wished to deflect from themselves any backlash concerning an irregular Royal liaison with one of their community.

Although the new Clandestine Marriages Act had already been passed and had received the Royal Assent in June 1753, it was not due on the statute books until Lady Day, 25th March 1754. So it was not yet in force on 11th December 1753, when Hannah Lightfoot married Isaac Axford, and the Mayfair Chapel was still therefore a legal location for a marriage. The fact that 'Dr' Keith had been excommunicated by the Church of England and was not licensed to carry out marriages, was not relevant since the 'ceremony' was actually carried out by one of his assistants. So, whilst this marriage was neither a Quaker ceremony nor was it conducted at The Friends' House or any other specifically authorised place, it was nevertheless perfectly legal and binding.

There is no direct evidence concerning who it was that Hannah ran off with, nor where to, since she was in a closed coach that made a clean escape from her pursuing husband.

The only clue is the story that, approaching some gates, the coachman called out 'Royal Family' to get the gates opened and avoid having to stop to pay the toll. But after her disappearance Mrs Axford (the name she seems to have used where necessary) is known to have lived in secret locations in Peckham, in Knightsbridge, in Hampstead, and in Tottenham. Her portrait was painted at least twice by Joshua Reynolds, the leading portraitist of the day, in which she is dressed in rich silks. One, entitled simply 'Mrs Axford', is on display at Knole House, Sevenoaks, in Kent under the catalogue title *Mrs Axford, the Fair Quaker*. Another, very similar, is just called *Portrait of a Lady*. The information Reynolds was given to decide on these titles would have been entered in his 'Sitters' books together with other interesting information such as his fees, dates, and particularly, the name of the person(s) who commissioned the paintings. Unfortunately, these details are in those books that just happen to be missing from the collection he left behind. But someone rich, powerful and with great influence must have been behind all this, to have maintained her so richly, to pay the fees of the likes of Joshua Reynolds, and to have been able to hide the lady so completely. Prince George fits that bill, except that he had shown no previous aptitude for any intrigues of this sort.

Hannah declared in her Will that she bore George three children, two sons and a daughter, but very little information is known of any of them, not even who they were. It is not known how old she was when she died, nor where she had been living at the time, though there is a persistent story concerning a grave in an Islington church cemetery. The headstone of this grave bears the name 'Rebecca Powell' and the date of death given is 27ᵗʰ May 1759. The story is that this grave actually contains the remains of Hannah Lightfoot. It is said that the funeral and interment of this person, whoever she was, was carried out secretly, at dawn, by the Rev. Zachary Brooke who, at the time, was Chaplain to George II. Brooke apparently did have a niece called Rebecca Powell, and the inscription on the tombstone refers to a 'chaste maiden' of twenty-three. But why would this niece have been buried there so secretively, at such an hour, and without any other mourners being present? And why, as Royal Chaplain, did Brooke undertake such a furtive proceeding anyway unless the deceased was someone who, equally secretively, had been of importance to a high-ranking 'royal'? And was it just coincidence that, a few years later on his retirement, Brooke was awarded not just one but three livings by order of King George III? Could this indeed be the grave of Hannah Lightfoot? The documents in the Public Records Office show that Hannah Lightfoot, then aged twenty nine, married the Prince of Wales, in a second ceremony, *on that very day of 27ᵗʰ May 1759* and if these documents are to be believed, this would have been a pretty good trick for a dead woman. This Islington grave story is an example of the many that have accrued around this young woman who ran off with and then secretly married the Prince of Wales, bore him children who *could* have been his legitimate heirs, and then just completely disappeared. As to the matter of *where* she died, the highly-respected Family History Library of the Church of the Latter Day Saints (the worldwide genealogical database of the Mormons) which is the largest of its kind in the world, states simply that she died in Pennsylvania, though not even an estimated date is offered. Many of the early English Quakers had established a settlement there so this is a feasible place for her to have gone to, whether voluntarily or by 'persuasion', and of course being there would explain how she managed so completely to disappear.

She had been brought up in a strictly religious household with a very rigid code of behaviour. George, his teenage hormones aside, strongly disliked the womanising practices of his father the late Prince Frederick, his uncles, and his grandfather King George II. A precept drummed into him by his mother, Princess Augusta, was 'George, be a king' and this he intended to do, but not a king such as his grandfather had been, nor even a prince in the mould of his father and uncles. Although following their elopement, he and Hannah knew that they could not marry since she was already married, it is clear that if they were ever able to legitimise their relationship, they would both want to do so at once.

And in 1759, after five years as his mistress, George and Hannah did secretly marry, at Kew Chapel, on 17th April, reconfirming the ceremony on 27th May, at Peckham. Hannah, knowing that she had legally married Isaac Axford, would not have deliberately contracted a second and bigamous marriage, with George or anyone else. (He, on the other hand, would possibly have had only a little problem in marrying Hannah even if she were still married to Axford, since he was to marry Queen Charlotte just a couple of years later). But the Lightfoot/Axford marriage had never been consummated, and was thus null and void, even though a formal decree of annulment had not been issued. It was obviously impossible for Hannah to obtain a decree without simultaneously disclosing her whereabouts and creating a *cause célèbre*, and Axford, who could have obtained one without a problem, had not done so. He in fact had done nothing about his marriage, even though he could have just as easily have obtained a divorce for desertion. Perhaps he simply wanted to make life difficult for George and Hannah by denying her the 'comfort' of a divorce. But after more than five years Prince George clearly felt able to approach the Rev. Dr James Wilmot, a cleric often seen at Court, and ask him about a marriage to Hannah Lightfoot. Equally clearly, Wilmot, who was certainly no Alexander Keith, felt able to accept the fact of the non-consummation as an annulment and formalise their relationship by marrying them. Isaac Axford too might have regarded this fact of non-consummation as an annulment, but at his own marriage later that same year to his cousin Miss Bartlett, he described himself as a widower, so perhaps he had heard, and believed the story about the Islington grave. Its date of May 1759 was very convenient for his marriage seven months later in December.

But did Dr Wilmot *in fact* marry George and Hannah? And if so, when? While the evidence (the certificates of their marriage) lies in the Public Records Office, the inability to carry out forensic testing necessitates demonstration that the marriage of George's brother Henry, Duke of Cumberland, to his Duchess, Anne Horton, was invalid. For the documentation on the marital affairs of these two brothers had become deeply enmeshed.

Although rumours about George and Hannah had been around since he first eloped with her, the documentation that might give substance to them only began to appear after his death more than 60 years later in 1820. Specific claims were then being made concerning the marriage of the late Duke of Cumberland to Anne Horton, claims which for good reason could not have been made in the King's lifetime. These claims were that Cumberland had gone through a ceremony of marriage with Anne Horton whilst he was already married to Dr Wilmot's daughter Olive, who was not only then still living but pregnant with his child. That King George had actively assisted in covering up his brother's bigamy and the Olive Wilmot problem. And that he had also made generous arrangements for the unborn child's financial and social future. Documents demonstrating the proofs of these arrangements, and of this alleged first marriage of Cumberland's existed. But they were not published until after (for some documents, many years after,) the King's death in 1820. Mrs Olive (Wilmot) Serres, the Duke of Cumberland's daughter by Olive Wilmot, the owner of these documents, had absolutely no interest in the Lightfoot marriage. Her concern was solely to prove the Cumberland/Wilmot marriage since she claimed to be the daughter of that union and wanted her inheritance of both royal status and money that had been ordered, according to these documents, by King George III. The difficulty was that this first Cumberland marriage could not really be proved without, *at the same time,* demonstrating that King George *had* married Hannah Lightfoot prior to his marriage to Princess Charlotte, and no-one really wanted to run that particular hare. The constitutional consequences of that disclosure were to be avoided if at all possible.

The following documents are among the many bearing on the George/Hannah affair, which are in the Public Records Office:

1. April 17, 1759

   The marriage of these parties was this day duly solemnised at Kew Chapel according to the rites and ceremonies of the Church of England by myself.

   George P.   J. Wilmot

   Hannah

   Witness to this marriage

   W. Pitt.

   Anne Tayler.

2. May 27, 1759

   This is to certify that the marriage of these parties (George, Prince of Wales, to Hannah Lightfoot) was duly solemnised this day, according to the rites and ceremonies of the Church of England, at their residence at Peckham, by myself.

   George Guelph   J. Wilmot

   Hannah Lightfoot

   Witness to the marriage of these parties–

   William Pitt.

   Anne Tayler

3. I certify that George Prince of Wales married Hannah Wheeler alias Lightfoot April 17th 1759 but from finding the latter to be her right name I solemnised the union of the said parties a second time May the 27th 1759 as the Certificate affixed to this paper will confirm.

Wilmot

Jan 1st 1789

I solemnly certify that I married George Prince of Wales by two distinct solemnizations owing to the doubts as to the name Princess Hannah went by previous to her marriage, which will account for these Certificates closely following each other.   Wilmot

'W. Pitt' in the first document was the same 'William Pitt' in the second, who was also the great statesman and future Earl of Chatham and who, as 'Chatham' also witnessed many of the other documents in this affair. Anne Tayler is thought to have been the former maid in the Wheeler household who probably encouraged Hannah in George's courtship.

4. Hampstead. 7 July 1762

Provided I depart this life, I commend my two sons, and my daughter to the kind protection of their Royal Father, my Husband, His Majesty King George III, bequeathing whatever property I die possessed of to such dear offspring of my ill fated marriage. In case of the death of each of my children, I give and bequeath to Olive Wilmot, daughter of my best friend, Doctor Wilmot, whatever property I am entitled to or possessed of at the time of my death.

(Signed):   Hannah Regina.

Witness: J. Dunning

                                        William Pitt

The signature, (Hannah *Regina*), clearly demonstrates Hannah's view of her legitimate status. The date indicates that she was still living in 1762, when she would have been approaching her 32nd birthday.

Later, stories would surface that, with George showing an interest in a young lady at Court, and with his advisors concerned that he should effect a 'suitable' marriage, Hannah Lightfoot was spirited away (to Pennsylvania?) George would perhaps be persuaded that she had died and been buried under another name (perhaps 'Rebecca Powell'?), deliberately to keep secret any reference to the affair and supposedly to ease his conscience. Whilst something like this might explain her total disappearance and also give a decent cover to the King's subsequent actions, it could not account for the evidence from the documents that were to come to light. Nor of course could it explain the stories about her presumed children by George, all of whom appear to have been born after she was supposed to have died.

The Rev. Dr James Wilmot MA, DD

Dr James Wilmot

James Wilmot is a central character in both the Hannah Lightfoot story and its principal sub-plot concerning the Duke of Cumberland's daughter; always discreetly in the background, his presence is felt at most of the significant events in this story. He was born in 1726, went to Trinity College Oxford, where he gained an MA and DD, (quite unlike 'Dr' Keith), and became a Fellow (ultimately the Senior Fellow) of the College. And he is supposed to have lived a quiet, celibate life as an Oxford Don.

Except that Mrs Olive Wilmot Serres, his niece *or* as she later claimed, his granddaughter, said and later provided documents alleged to show that he did marry, had a daughter (her mother), frequently stayed in London, was a familiar figure at Court, and was a confidant of influential and powerful people. And in support of this alternative lifestyle one may note that this supposedly quiet and retiring Fellow and cleric had clearly made himself something of an international reputation with views which he shared with William Pitt and others, in opposing King George's treatment of the American Colonists; for in the year of his death in 1807 a small town in the State of New Hampshire in America was re-named *Wilmot* in honour of his support for the Colonists' cause.

Origin: Originally a part of New London, Wilmot was carved out of the gore of Mount Kearsage and incorporated in 1807. It was named in honour of Dr. James Wilmot, a scholar and clergyman, and rector at Barton-on-Heath in Warwickshire, England. Dr. Wilmot had joined with William Pitt, the Marquis of Rockingham, and others. in protesting the treatment of the American colonies by the British crown.

Taken from the official web-site of Wilmot, New Hampshire

The Wilmot family traced its history and name back to Norman times to one of William the Conqueror's nobles named de Villemot. Previous generations of Wilmots had served at Court, one of James's ancestors being the well-known John Wilmot, 2nd Earl of Rochester, who was a member of the so-called 'court of wits' around King Charles II. Rochester is regarded as having been one of the wittiest (and certainly the most sexually explicit) poets in the English language. His daughter, Lady Anne Wilmot, married Francis

Greville, and their grandson Francis became Earl of Warwick in 1759; Francis' son George (Lord Brooke) succeeded to his title. This George is the Earl of Warwick who appears in these pages; he was thus distantly related to Dr Wilmot and to Mrs Olive Serres.

Lord George Brooke, later Earl of Warwick, had been a very wealthy man who was also a profligate spender (much of it being on improvements to his great castle) and gambler. One day at the tables in 1776 he lost a particularly large sum that he could ill-afford. Mr Vernon, his creditor on this occasion, having three attractive daughters and an eye for their future, is said to have suggested that if Warwick would choose one of them for his wife, the debt could be converted into a dowry. Warwick had previously been married to Georgiana Peachey in 1771, but she died in childbirth exactly a year later, so in 1776 he was both eligible and interested. The deal was agreed and Warwick, having married Henrietta Vernon, was able to resume his expensive lifestyle though he was later forced to hand over control of his estates to a Trust after again bringing his family close to ruin. His eldest son, now grown up, gained control of the family estates and Trust and succeeded in restoring the family finances but, according to Mrs Serres in her *Letters from the Earl of Warwick to Mrs Olive Wilmot Serres*, kept his father virtually penniless, completely refusing to let him have an allowance saying 'What does he want with money? He has everything found that he wants.' And 'What can I do? If I meet my father's wishes, what will become of my mother? She will be again reduced to beggary.' His father, who frequently wrote to Mrs

Serres, would rail at both his wife and his son for their refusals to let him have money, saying he had not even a sixpence in his pocket.

In his own day James Wilmot's relative, his uncle Sir Edward Wilmot, had been physician to King George II, to Frederick, Prince of Wales, and also for a brief period to King George III; he was very probably the source of James Wilmot's introduction to the Court. It was Sir Edward who informed George III of his grandfather's dying wish that his body should be embalmed with a double quantity of perfume and then laid close to that of his late wife Queen Caroline.

Whilst he was a student at Oxford, Wilmot, according to Mrs Serres, became friendly with a Polish fellow student Stanislaus Poniatowski (who later became King Stanislaus, the last King of Poland). Through this friendship, Mrs Serres said, Wilmot met and then secretly married (the Hannah Lightfoot story is all about secret marriages) Stanislaus' sister, a Polish princess who was in Oxford with him, and had a daughter by her (Olive) who later married the King's brother, the Duke of Cumberland. Through the marriage of his daughter to Cumberland, this marriage of Wilmot's has some significance in these events, yet most of the details Mrs Serres relates of it are simply not true; they appear to have been drawn from her own imagination, based on some notes she found in his papers after his death. They gave a lot of trouble years later, to her own daughter in the notorious trial of June 1866.

Stanislaus Poniatowski, in 1764 was elected King of Poland, the last King as it turned out, though his only effective rival was an uncle and the election was a strictly family affair. He did *not* study at Oxford, so he could not have become friendly with Wilmot through that route; although he was in England for much of 1754, he spent just one day in Oxford. He did have two sisters, Ludwika (b.1728) and Izabela (b.1730); however they both married Polish aristocrats, in 1746 and 1748 respectively, and each girl was just eighteen at the time of her marriage. So how, other than in Mrs Serres' imagination, could this Wilmot marriage to a Polish princess (which he himself attests *did* take place) have happened? Dr Wilmot confirms in affidavits only that he married a 'Princess of Poland' and that he had a daughter by her; he identifies the Princess no further than by saying she was a sister of the King of Poland. He does not give the where or the when of the marriage, how he met her, nor even her name, though on this there can be only two possibilities.

For such a marriage to have occurred these dates suggest it would have to have been around 1746/7, when Wilmot would have been twenty or twenty one; this really sets up the younger sister, Izabela, as the candidate for a secret, and *very* brief marriage. The secrecy, said Mrs Serres, was necessary to protect the princess because Royalty were only supposed to marry other Royalty; this was an obviously silly piece of nonsense, particularly for an elected Royalty. A more compelling reason for secrecy might have been that Trinity College Fellows were debarred from marrying during the time of their Fellowship, on pain of losing that honour and privilege.

However Wilmot wasn't elected to a Fellowship until 1753 (though he was a probationer Fellow in 1752) so that could not have been a valid reason either for the secrecy. Whatever the reason however, this Polish princess, having made her appearance, seems then to have disappeared almost as completely as did Hannah Lightfoot, making only a fleeting re-appearance some years later at the time of her supposed daughter's marriage. So did Wilmot actually have a wife? What happened to her? Who brought up the daughter of this supposed marriage? The marriage story is clearly relevant to this enquiry since a key character is Olive Wilmot Serres, who claimed that her mother was the product of it, but to be believable there has to be something more than this.

The Poniatowskis were a branch of the Czartoryscy family which effectively ruled Poland and its institutions for some three generations and which, with all its branches was collectively known as 'The Family'; its members, through their dynastic links with the earlier royal House of Jagiello were all ranked as Princes and Princesses. 'The Family', its women as much as the men, led very liberated lives even by today's standards: for instance three of Stanislaus' cousins (all sisters) married and divorced so frequently that it was said that between them they had gone the round of the entire Polish peerage. One member of the 'Family', a widow, was said to have supported a whole army of dependants through bestowing her favours on five successive Russian ambassadors. Another cousin was reputed to be, simultaneously, the mistress of both Stanislaus and a friend of his. Stanislaus himself, during a year-long visit to Russia, was the lover of the Empress Catherine; it was her direct influence that later ensured his election as King.

Given the family lifestyle quite clearly Izabela, then aged about sixteen, *might* have visited England, met Wilmot at the Court in London where she would no doubt have had an entré, and then too hastily married him, perhaps insisting on secrecy to protect herself from the family consequences of what would clearly be regarded as a rash and unsuitable marriage. She, after all, was a Catholic Polish aristocrat from a very wealthy and powerful family, whilst he was just a Protestant English student priest. Perhaps too, news of a proposal from a much more suitable Polish aristocrat would have led her to abandon her Wilmot marriage and return home for an easy divorce which, given the record of her three cousins, would clearly not have been a problem, leaving her daughter with its father.

This is pure speculation but it's the sort of scenario that could have been played out. As far as Wilmot was concerned he might have been unwilling to recognise the divorce and have regarded himself as still married to her. Perhaps too, embarrassment at his situation might have given him a reason to keep the marriage secret. (Also, even though he was not elected to a Fellowship till 1753, if he had Fellowship ambitions he would have been ineligible for election, or later deprived of it were it to become known that he was married.) Then, if we suppose that the baby daughter of this brief marriage was given to his sister to raise, this little mystery can be explained whilst retaining all its essential points. A difficulty with this scenario is that Wilmot's sister Olive (this was clearly the favoured name for Wilmot women) didn't marry Captain Payne until 1754, when she was twenty six, so she may have had a few problems as a single woman explaining her acquisition of a baby. There is no indication however that Stanislaus was ever in England other than during 1754. Equally there is no evidence that Wilmot ever visited Poland, nor any evidence on how the supposed child of this supposed marriage was raised. Wilmot himself offers only the following information in the various documents located at the Public Records Office:

5. 1st January 1780.
    I solemnly certify that I privately was married to the Princess of Poland, the sister of the King of Poland but an unhappy Family difference induced us to keep our union secret.

Although this is dated 1st January 1780, he does not provide a date for the marriage. There is no reference here as to what the family problem was, (though the speculation above offers a possible insight), nor to his wife's name, nor to any offspring of this marriage. However, he acknowledges his daughter in the following notes:

6. I solemnly certify that I married the Princess of Poland and had Legitimate Issue Olive my Dear Daughter married March 4th 1767 to Henry Frederick Duke of Cumberland Brother of His Majesty George The Third who have issue Olive my supposed niece Born at Warwick April 3rd 1772.
    G. R.   J Wilmot
                                                 Robt. Wilmot
                                                 Chatham

And in another undated note, a kind of diary note, which must have been written sometime in March/April 1767, he wrote:

7. Olive my daughter Duchess of Cumberland received from her uncle King Stanislaus £5,000 presented privately by my wife Princess of Poland March the 9ᵗʰ 1767 with a case of diamonds. The ring for my -sister, Payne, and the box for Robert.
   To be at Oxford on the 10ᵗʰ.
   My brother Bob to meet me &c. on the 11th.
   Δ *C*8 11 L ☐ X D L ☐ T. –
   Lords C and S to be answered on the 17ᵗʰ.

      And on the reverse side

To pay C.W.P. the natural son of Lord C. £50 for his board &c.
To go to Bruton Street on the 15ᵗʰ to meet Lords P. and W.
To preach at A. on the 30ᵗʰ.
To be at R. on the 31ˢᵗ.
Lady P. to meet at E. on the 1ˢᵗ of June.

In the first entry of this note, he again acknowledges having both a wife and a daughter. In his mind at least, he is clearly still married. He states that his wife, his 'Princess of Poland', which perhaps out of vanity is the only way he ever refers to her, was in England on 9ᵗʰ March 1767, delivering wedding gifts to her daughter, who had married the Duke of Cumberland just five days earlier. This implies some kind of continued contact between himself and 'the Princess' for her to have been.informed of the marriage and deciding to visit. The meaning of the line of symbols, numbers and letters in the 'diary' note is not clear.

However, apart from his own notes such as those quoted, there is no independent evidence that Dr Wilmot ever married anyone, Polish princess or not. Nor any later account of how, or when, his supposed daughter Olive was introduced into Court circles, though given his own apparent intimacy there, this would clearly not have been a problem. All one can additionally say about this marriage is that Wilmot does not seem to have been the sort of man who would first invent such stories about himself and then keep them all a secret.

Olive Wilmot grew into a charming, intelligent young woman, attracting the attentions in particular of the Earl of Warwick and of the King's youngest brother Henry, Duke of Cumberland, both of whom wished to marry her. Warwick later certified (in one of Mrs Serres' documents now at the Public Records Office), that he had returned from the Continent specifically to propose marriage to her. He gave way in this contest to Cumberland, and Dr Wilmot officiated at the resulting private marriage. King George was said to have been present though he did not act as a witness. A few years later, when Cumberland contracted a second marriage (Olive was not only still living and married to him but also pregnant with their child, a girl who would also be called Olive), George was appalled. To protect his brother from a bigamy charge, and of course perhaps himself, since he was now 'married' to Princess Charlotte, he arranged that Olive and her as yet unborn child were swiftly and quietly put aside. However, Dr Wilmot was influential enough to ensure that appropriate documentation recording the facts concerning his daughter's marriage and his granddaughter's origins were signed by the King. (These are also PRO documents; see Appendix 1, Nos: 5,10,11,12,13,15,16). Wilmot was no doubt in a position to achieve this because of his intimate knowledge of the King's own similar marital situation, having officiated at the then Prince of Wales' own secret marriage to Hannah Lightfoot a few years previously. Mrs Olive Serres' account of Wilmot's supposed secret marriage to his Polish princess and his intimate involvement in Royal secrets, together with supporting certificates and attestations were all, however, quite at odds with what had always been thought to be the quiet life of the Rev. Dr James Wilmot, the Oxford Don and intellectual.

In 1787 he retired and was awarded the Living of Barton-on-the-Heath, a small parsonage in Warwickshire in the gift of Trinity College, where he was Rector until his death in 1807. A couple of years before he died however, he instructed his servants to collect together most of his papers and, in a great bonfire outside his house, burn them. At the time this was a quite mysterious action. But seen from a viewpoint of 200 years later, this might be regarded as an indication of the considerable discretion which made him such a valued and trusted courtier.

An interesting sidelight on Dr Wilmot is that in the final period of his life during his retirement, he embarked upon a study of William Shakespeare and spent some four years in the early 1780s scouring the countryside within a wide radius of Stratford-on-Avon in search of any literary legacy, such as letters to or from Shakespeare, or a book—any book—that could be shown to have once been owned by the Bard. He couldn't find a single thing. The implications of this so shocked him that he kept it to himself, together with his growing belief that the Bard could not have been Shakespeare but must have been Francis Bacon; it was only some years later that he confided this theory to an acquaintance, James Cowell. This, subsequently, became the subject of a paper presented to the Ipswich Philosophical Society by Cowell, who acknowledged Dr Wilmot's work; and thus was started the thriving *Who was Shakespeare?* industry. Dr Wilmot is now regarded as the virtual founder of the Francis Bacon Society.

The Duke of Cumberland

Henry Frederick
Duke of Cumberland

Anne Horton

Henry's and George's father, Frederick Prince of Wales, who was the heir to King George II, had nine legitimate children from his marriage to Princess Augusta of Saxe-Gotha-Altenburg (he also had two illegitimate children, by different women). Frederick died in 1751 aged only 44, thoroughly unloved by both his mother and the Nation, after being hit on the head by a cricket ball. His nature, and his relationship with his parents were such that Queen Caroline said of him:

"My dearest first born is the greatest ass, and the greatest liar, and the greatest canaille, and the greatest beast in the whole world and I most heartily wish he was out of it."

When, after the cricket ball incident his mother's wish was granted, the National sentiment on the event was expressed in the following verse:

"Here lies Fred who was alive and now is dead.
Had it been his father I had much rather,
Had it been his sister nobody would have missed her,
Had it been his brother, still better than another,
Had it been the whole generation, so much better for the nation,
But since it is Fred who was alive and is now dead,
There is no more to be said."

Frederick left to his eldest son George the title of Prince of Wales and the succession to the throne. His second youngest son was Henry Frederick, Duke of Cumberland (1745-1790), who married Lady Anne Horton (she was the widow of Mr Christopher Horton but being also the daughter of the Earl of Carhampton was entitled to the honorific 'Lady') whilst already married to Olive Wilmot. Olive, the child of his first, and legitimate, marriage was born some six months after he had contracted the second marriage. Later, as Mrs Olive Wilmot Serres, this child was to become the key figure in all investigations into the Hannah Lightfoot marriage; she also became the mother of Mrs Lavinia Ryves whose legal action in 1866 could have determined forever the truth about Hannah Lightfoot. But because of the way in which that trial was conducted it succeeded only, despite its definitive outcome, in ensuring the survival of the mystery.

These were the circumstances (detailed, and with supporting documentation—see Appendix 1—provided by Mrs Olive Serres) concerning that first marriage: At 9:00 pm in the evening of 4th March 1767 Henry Frederick, Duke of

Cumberland married Olive Wilmot, daughter of the well-regarded courtier the Rev. Dr James Wilmot. This was a private ceremony at the house of Lord Archer, a long-standing friend of Wilmot's, in Grosvenor Square, London. The marriage was performed by Dr Wilmot, and those said to have been present included King George and William Pitt, who had recently been raised to the peerage as the Earl of Chatham. Two certificates were written, one on the wedding day itself simply signed by 'J Wilmot' stating he had performed the marriage, and a second six weeks later attesting to the marriage but now with the witness signatures of Brooke (Warwick) and Addez, with additional signatures of Chatham and Dunning. These Certificates are among those in the PRO collection, and copies are included in Appendix 1 (Nos 4,7,8,9).

The marriage was private and low-key, perhaps because of King George's antipathy to the idea that members of his immediate family should marry subjects. Four and a half years later, on 2nd October 1771 and whilst this marriage was seemingly running smoothly Cumberland married again, secretively, now to the widowed Mrs Anne Horton, sister of the well-known and controversial soldier/politician Colonel Luttrel. Walpole, in his *Memoirs* said of Anne Horton that she was 'the Duke of Grafton's Mrs Horton, the Duke of Dorset's Mrs Horton, everyone's Mrs Horton'. He thought she was 'pretty rather than handsome, with the air of a lady of pleasure rather than a woman of quality'; and that 'her coquetry was so active, so varied, and yet so habitual, that it was difficult not to see through it, and just as difficult to resist.' Others have commented on her free use of coarse language. He described Cumberland as 'a weak and debauched boy' who paraded his women, usually other men's wives, with careless bravado; earlier in 1771 Cumberland had been forced to appeal to the King for help in paying £10,000 damages and £3,000 costs for having 'criminal conversation with' (ie seducing) the wife of Lord Grosvenor.

For George, this marriage was an outrage. He received the news of it when Cumberland went to him and, walking in the garden, gave him a letter. The King took it saying, he supposed he need not read it now. 'Yes, Sir' said the Duke, 'You must read it directly.' Having read it, George reacted with considerable anger: 'You fool, you blockhead, you villain, you had better have debauched all the unmarried girls in England, you had better have committed adultery with all the married women, but this woman can be nothing—she shall never be anything. Go abroad 'til I am determined what to do.' Cumberland and his new bride went abroad for a year and on their return Anne Horton was allowed the title of Duchess, though not of Princess, and was banned for life from George's Court. This somewhat extreme reaction was, however, not just to Mrs Horton. It was, of course, a grave discourtesy by his brother not to have informed the King. Not only was the lady a subject, and thus almost by definition 'unsuitable' according to George's ideas, but she herself was also personally very unsuitable, as both Walpole's and the King's remarks suggested. Worse, her brother, whose lifestyle included many mistresses, had a reputation for personal behaviour that did him no favours; his even occasional presence at Court could be a source of major embarrassments. (It has been said that the Duke only married Anne because her brother had threatened him with a duel if he didn't; Luttrell was supposedly protecting his sister's honour!) But worst of all, this marriage created a serious bigamy issue, and not just for George's brother but also, potentially, for the King himself.

Cumberland's response to his brother's anger, it has been said, was effectively to blackmail him into supporting a cover-up by suggesting that if he, Cumberland, were exposed then he would expose George's marriage to Hannah Lightfoot and thus create a huge scandal that would have incalculable consequences both for the Hanovers and the country. Blackmail or not, it was a possibility that was unthinkable. King George had no choice, and swift action was taken. Olive Wilmot was quietly taken out of circulation; she was three months pregnant at the time and in due course gave birth to a daughter, also called Olive, on 3rd April 1772. The birth and baptism were recorded by Dr Wilmot, and witnessed by his younger brother Robert, by Lord Chatham, and by a Mr J Dunning (a very successful lawyer who was later Solicitor General and a witness to many of the documents in this case). Coincidentally, Robert Wilmot's wife had just given birth to a stillborn child and the opportunity was taken the following day, 4th April, to give the baby to Mr and Mrs Robert Wilmot to bring up as their own. This is confirmed by a note in the PRO files, from the King, dated 4th April, to Lord Chatham (see Appendix 1, Nos 13,14,).

It happened that soon after this Cumberland affair the King learned that another of his brothers, the Duke of Gloucester, had been secretly married for several years to Lady Maria Waldegrave [Horace Walpole's niece, the illegitimate daughter of his elder brother]; George had always believed her to be just his brother's mistress. In May 1773, when Maria was imminently due to give birth to her first child by the Duke [she already had three by an earlier marriage] he wrote to his brother King George requesting that his marriage should be urgently recognised and formalised for the sake of this unborn child.

Acceding to this request, on 21ˢᵗ May 1773 the King instructed his Privy Council immediately to investigate the legality of the Gloucester marriage and, more to the point here, *at the same time* to inquire into the legality of the marriage of another brother, the Duke of Cumberland. The very next day three senior members of the Council—the Archbishop of Canterbury, the Bishop of London, and the Lord Chancellor—called on the Duke of Gloucester and took statements from him, his wife, and others swearing to the marriage. The following day [23ʳᵈ May] they called on the Duke of Cumberland and obtained from him the following declaration:

I, Henry Frederick Duke of Cumberland solemnly declare that I was married to the Honourable Anne Horton, Widow, on the second day of October One Thousand Seven Hundred and Seventy One, in the afternoon between the Hours of six and eight, at her house in Hertford Street, by William Stevens,

Clerk, Fellow of St. John's College in Cambridge, according to the Rites and Ceremonies of the Church of England, in the presence of Miss Elizabeth Luttrell, no other person being present. (signed) Henry.

Similar statements were taken from Anne, from the Clerk, and from Miss Luttrell. Questions (unrecorded) were asked and answers (also unrecorded) received. On the basis of these visits the Inquiry prepared first a 'draught' (*sic*) report then a final report declaring that on the basis of the evidence (ie the written declarations and the unrecorded answers) both Dukes had indeed married their respective ladies. There was however a significant difference between the draft and final reports. The *draft* stated that "a marriage was *legally* solemnised between the Duke of Cumberland and Anne Horton"; but the *final* report omitted the crucial word "legally" saying only that 'a marriage was solemnised...' This distinction also applied to the marriage of Duke of Gloucester and Maria Waldegrave. The King's instruction to the Council was to *inquire into the legality* of these marriages, and this they managed to avoid reporting on. But at least the King had, thanks to Gloucester's problem, been able to seize an opportunity to protect to some extent both Cumberland and himself from any later scandal over Cumberland's marriage to Mrs Horton. The Inquiry's final report was immediately accepted by the King in Council, so at least there were no questions to be asked about Maria's baby, which was born on the 29th May 1773. The documentation relating to this Inquiry can be seen at the Lambeth Palace Library.

The Olive Wilmot crisis was dealt with by these actions, although it is clear that Dr Wilmot would not have been thrilled by the way his daughter was treated. However, thanks to his intimate knowledge of and involvement in these secret affairs of State he was able to ensure both financial provision and documentation of origin for his granddaughter. (See Appendix 1, Nos: 17,21). Of his daughter, Olive, he recorded that she died, in December 1774, of a broken heart (Appendix 1: No 19).

Probably the King didn't need to have his arm twisted very hard on this as he was extremely angry at his brother's action and presumably very understanding of Wilmot's anger. Amongst the financial arrangements, a very substantial legacy of £15,000 (Appendix 1, No: 17) was willed by the King for the baby. But because it was never actually paid, this legacy became part of Mrs Serres' claims; and later her daughter Mrs Ryves claimed in the 1866 trial that, as Cumberland's granddaughter, she was then the legitimate heir to this legacy.

The Duke and Duchess of Cumberland, returning from their year's exile, settled down to a life of hedonistic pleasure away from the Royal Court, from which of course the Duchess had been permanently banned, and seem not to have troubled King or Country again. He was a son worthy of his father. It was Olive, his daughter by his early marriage to Olive Wilmot who, by her efforts to prove her parentage, has effectively kept this rather useless man's name alive.

George III

George, Prince of Wales

George was the first of the Hanovers to be a real 'English' king in that he was the first to have been born and brought up in England and to speak English rather than German. He was also the first to rebel against the amorality and licentiousness that was such a feature of the Hanover dynasty.

In his childhood George did not distinguish himself in any way that would please his grandfather King George II, who thought him good for reading the bible to his mother, and not much else. His brother Edward, to whom he was close, was more to their grandfather's taste, as the following schoolroom story suggests:

"When you and I are grown" said Edward to George, "You shall take a wife, and I shall keep a mistress". Their mother Princess Augusta, hastily putting a stop to wherever this

discussion might lead, told him "You had better learn your pronouns. I believe you do not know what a pronoun is".
Edward: "I know what it is. A pronoun is to a noun what a mistress is to a wife — a substitute and a representative."

George, who at least in his first two decades was not renowned for his ability to think on his feet, at least knew he did not want to be a king in the mould of his predecessors; he was also continually being impressed by his mother that he should not only reign but govern. In his 'teen' years he formed a very strong link, which lasted for about a decade, to the Earl of Bute, an ambitious politician who was also reputedly the lover of the by then widowed Princess Augusta (an attractive woman, Augusta was only nineteen years older than her eldest son).

The influence that Augusta exercised over the young Prince was considerable. His grandfather wanted to weaken this influence, so with the agreement of the Government assigned him an annual allowance of £40,000 to set up and run his own independent household. George consulted with his mother, accepted the money, but remained within her household. Lord Bute's influence too over George was such that on his accession in October 1760, George immediately appointed Bute as a member of the Privy Council, and then just a month later appointed him First Gentleman of the Bedchamber. Even though he held only these Household appointments, Bute was so influential that George had to engineer a government position for him by dismissing one of his Secretaries of State and appointing Bute in his place.

Between them, Princess Augusta and the Earl of Bute were for a few years able to steer George's thinking in the directions they felt most appropriate.

Despite his dislike of his family's sexual behaviour, the young George's strong sensuality meant that by 1760/1 he was already creating gossip concerning his attentions, and possible intentions, towards an attractive young girl still only in her 'teens, Lady Sarah Lennox. Even with his strong feelings for this girl, however, he was persuaded by Bute that he should not marry one of his subjects; only marriage to a foreign princess would do. Bute sent an envoy to visit the Courts of Europe looking for a suitable bride, who would be a Protestant, virginal, and perhaps have a dowry. And so George allowed himself to be led into marriage with Princess Charlotte Sophia of Mecklenburgh-Strelitz, reputedly the plainest woman in Europe. Aside from his teenage passion for Hannah Lightfoot, which in one sense could be regarded as a sowing of wild oats, George's strong sense of moral rectitude, his determination not to follow the way of life of his family, allied to his equally strong physical needs, meant that Charlotte, plain as she might be, would over the next twenty one years obligingly provide him with fifteen children.

One of the objections to the likelihood of George's affair with Hannah is its sheer unlikeliness. He, the heir to the Throne, living in a sophisticated Court; she at the time, half as old again as him, a naïve young woman living in a very restrictive enclosed environment. Yet George, who had a quiet and religious disposition, was brought up in an amoral Court full of colourfully dressed ladies always ready to display themselves. It was a Court where the level of conversation was such that it enabled the witticism of young Prince Edward in the schoolroom. It was a Court that was also full of stories concerning his mother's relationship with her close friend and adviser Lord Bute. (One of these stories was that when Princess Augusta scolded Elizabeth Chudleigh over her way of life, Miss Chudleigh supposedly responded with '*Chacun à son Bute*'). So it was quite possibly the quiet and sober appearance of the pretty Quaker girl, so much older than him but also with a strong religious side to her, that appealed. Perhaps he came initially to regard her almost as a goddess, a divinity whom he could worship, just as so many other teenage boys have tended to regard attractive older women both before and after his time. Equally, Hannah Lightfoot, with her plain and sober Quaker background, might well have found quite irresistible this elegantly dressed self-confident young man who, although not sharing her religion could, nevertheless, share her religious outlook; a young man so different to any of the men she could have encountered in her otherwise very sheltered life. And in the ambitious and sophisticated Miss Elizabeth Chudleigh, George had the ideal person to arrange his meetings with the goddess.

Elizabeth Chudleigh

Miss Chudleigh

Born in 1720, Elizabeth was a beautiful though not wealthy young lady who quite early in life demonstrated a marked ability to attract well-born men of title, influence and substance. She grew up to be regarded as one of the most colourful women of her time. Her father, Colonel Chudleigh, was Lieutenant-Governor of The Royal Hospital at Chelsea; he had lost all his money in the South Sea Bubble but the family nevertheless lived comfortably on his salary thanks to the Grace & Favour House that went with the job. However he died when she was only seven years old, and the family had to move out of their house; Mrs Chudleigh decided to relocate to Devon where she had family.

As a young teenager in Devon, Elizabeth met the portraitist Joshua Reynolds, who was on a visit to his home county. He was so taken with her beauty that he asked permission to paint her portrait, and then to show it in London. It created such an impression there that he wrote to her saying that London wanted to meet the original. No sooner suggested, than she had arrived with her mother. She met the future Earl of Bath who took a strong interest in her; he was influential in getting her appointed, at nineteen, as a Maid of Honour to Augusta, then Princess of Wales and mother of the future George III. Soon after, Miss Chudleigh reached an understanding with the young Duke of Hamilton that was intended to lead to marriage. A prime mover in this arrangement was the Duke's aunt, Lady Archibald Hamilton, who was at the time the favoured mistress of Frederick, Prince of Wales. She was thought to be concerned to defend this position from such attractive new arrivals in Court as Elizabeth Chudleigh. The Duke soon afterwards went off to do the traditional tour of Europe, promising to write frequently to her. Following a slight illness Elizabeth returned to Devonshire to recover in the healthier country air, living with her aunt Mrs Hanmer, at the house of her cousin Mrs Merrill, in the village of Lainston. Mrs Hanmer, supposedly jealous of her sister's relative social success, and deciding that a duke was simply too good for her niece, intercepted and withheld all of Hamilton's letters. Elizabeth fretted about this apparent loss of interest in her particularly as, because he was travelling she had no address to which to write to him. In 1744, aged twenty four and disappointed at apparently losing Hamilton, she listened too much to her aunt and married, in effect on the rebound, the well-born but impoverished junior naval officer the Hon. Augustus Hervey, 2nd son of the Earl of Bristol; the marriage was kept secret since neither was well off and they could not afford for Elizabeth to lose her position as Maid of Honour. (It was an unwritten rule at Court that Maids of Honour must be unmarried women and, preferably, maidens, though this latter was a rule more honoured in the breach than the observance.) The Duke of Hamilton, on his eventual return, went on to marry one of the beautiful Gunning sisters who were by then the focus of attention at the Court

Lieutenant Hervey returned to sea duty and Miss Chudleigh returned to London and the Court. Two years later, in 1746, Hervey was back in England, and in the summer of 1747 Elizabeth secretly gave birth, in Chelsea, to a son who died after only a few months. On her return to the Court she found she was the subject of gossip concerning the cause of her recent absence. Once, challenging this, she asked the Earl of Chesterfield (the noted wit, and author of the well-known *Letters to his Son*) what he thought of the rumours that she had had twins: 'Madame' he told her 'I only ever believe the half of what I hear'. She became the talk of Society over her ever more scandalous conduct, which included her appearance at a masked ball in 1749 barely dressed, in the character of 'Iphigenia for the Sacrifice', giving rise to such comments as that she was 'so naked that the high priest might easily inspect the entrails of the victim'. She was quite a favourite (perhaps even more) of King George II, who gave her an expensive gift 'out of his own privy purse and not charged to the Civil List', and appointed her mother to a well-paid post as housekeeper at Windsor. Life had become significantly more comfortable.

The eventual death of her father-in-law, the Earl of Bristol, meant that her husband's elder brother now held the title, but he in turn was in frail health and was not expected to live too long. And being childless, *his* heir was his younger brother Augustus, Elizabeth's husband. She could now expect to become, in due course, the Countess of Bristol, which would be a further significant improvement in both status and fortune particularly since her husband had become a notably successful Naval Officer earning many promotions and much prize money.

By 1759/60 however Miss Chudleigh had earned for herself a big promotion; she was now the acknowledged mistress of the extremely rich Evelyn Pierrepoint, 2nd Duke of Kingston. She much preferred the idea of being a very wealthy Duchess rather than a reasonably well-off Countess, particularly since she no longer had any love for her husband and had hardly had any contact with him for many years. In order to marry her Duke, however, she needed to deal with the problem of an unwanted husband. He, after an active career at sea that had included many successful naval engagements, had finally left the Royal Navy in the rank of Vice-Admiral, and had entered politics. He wanted to be rid of his now notorious wife and favoured a divorce, but she didn't since she had never admitted to being married in the first place. Indeed so concerned had she been a few years earlier about this regrettable early marriage that she had even gone to some lengths to dispose of the documentary evidence that it had ever occurred, so a divorce would be a particularly awkward exercise to carry off. She persuaded her husband to agree to a procedure by which, in February 1769, she obtained a declaration that they had never been married, that she was and always had been Miss Elizabeth Chudleigh. One month later, aged forty-nine, she then married her Duke and, thereafter, was known as the Duchess of Kingston. The Duke died in July 1773, leaving a life interest in his entire estate to his widow, though on condition that she remained a widow since he was concerned that she might be vulnerable to any fortune-hunting adventurer(!). But in a challenge to this will Evelyn Meadows, the Duke's nephew, who was somewhat upset at being deprived of his inheritance, investigated the background to this supposed Chudleigh marital involvement with Hervey that had inevitably been aired. He was able to prove, in a trial at the House of Lords that attracted huge interest, that the Duchess had indeed entered into an early marriage to Augustus Hervey, by now Earl of Bristol. And that not only had this marriage had been valid, it still was because their 'separation' had been achieved by collusion. Her proper title was, therefore, Countess of Bristol. Her marriage to the Duke of Kingston was thus bigamous and, consequently, she was not entitled to the late Duke's estate, which then reverted to Evelyn Meadows. (The Duchess, as she continued to be known to the end of her life, had been in Rome when she heard of the action being taken against her and decided to return to England as soon as possible to defend her interests. The English banker who was looking after her money and valuables in Rome made serious difficulties about getting resources to her quickly enough. She returned to his office with a loaded pistol and was able to persuade him that he could indeed quite easily meet her needs.) That the trial was held in the House of Lords was a typical piece of Chudleigh arrogance and flamboyance: she simply insisted that since she would be proved to be either a Duchess or a Countess it was her right to be tried by her fellow Peers, being mistakenly confident that there were enough Lords still living who had enjoyed her favours sufficiently in the past to influence the outcome. Her Counsel included three Dukes, two Lords, and a plain Mr.

She escaped punishment, and went to Paris still in possession of a considerable fortune, quantities of jewellery, and several extremely valuable items from the Duke's estate. She travelled extensively around Europe and Russia. To smooth her path into Russian Society she sent ahead, as a gift to a member of the Court, a quite valuable pair of her late husband's paintings, but when she realised just how valuable they were, (a *Raphael* and a *Claude Lorrain*) she asked for them to be returned in exchange for a lesser pair. The recipient refused to oblige her. In Russia she became a favourite of the Czarina, received an offer of marriage from a Prince, and had many affairs. She made substantial investments there, including building a plant for the manufacture of brandy but, suddenly tiring of that country she gave everything to a carpenter she had taken a fancy to, and returned to Paris. There, she bought a house from the King's brother, but died suddenly at the age of sixty eight before she had finished paying for it. This then was the lady who, in her youth was procuress for Prince George in his wooing, and abduction on her wedding day, of Hannah Lightfoot.

Mrs Olive Serres

Olive Wilmot Serres

This lady is the key to the complete Hannah Lightfoot story. Born in 1772, she grew up as Miss Olive Wilmot, believing herself the daughter of Robert and Anna-Maria Wilmot, and niece of the Rev. Dr James Wilmot DD, Robert's elder brother. Robert had been County Treasurer in Warwick, but following a problem concerning some of the County's money had had to resign that post. His brother helped to set him up as a house painter in Paddington, West London, and also undertook to look after Robert's daughter Olive at the Rectory at Barton-on-the-Heath, the Living to which he had been appointed when he retired from Trinity College. She was a very imaginative girl, growing up to become an attractive and multi-talented young woman who wrote books, pamphlets, poetry, music (even a three act opera, 'The Castle of Avalon') and was also a skilled young painter. Some of her poems, together with the libretto of her opera, she later published in 1805 in *Flights of Fancy*. It has also been said that she appeared on the stage as 'Polly' in John Gay's *The Beggars Opera.* At seventeen she went to London where she studied painting and art under the fashionable John Thomas Serres, son of the well-known marine painter Dominic Serres; at nineteen she married him, after her father Robert had taken the necessary oath, since she was under age, that Olive was his legitimate daughter and that there were no objections to the marriage. The ceremony was performed by her uncle, Dr Wilmot, in his own church.

Mr and Mrs Serres returned to London but before long their differences caused them to separate and she set up on her own account as both a writer and painter, being successful enough as a painter to be exhibited at the Royal Academy. No fewer than twenty-seven of her paintings were shown at either the Royal Academy or the British Institution between 1793 and 1811. Her talent in this field was such that, in his substantial work *The Old English Landscape Painters,* Colonel M H Grant, who had an extremely low opinion of her as a woman, possibly due to the practices described below concerning her husband, nevertheless felt able to comment that

...[she] could not only paint, but paint well... Her canvasses, If in no sense masterpieces, are spirited pieces of work...

On the reverse of one her paintings of 1814 she described herself as 'Landscape Painter to the Prince Regent' and Grant notes: And such she undoubtedly was...

'Mountain Landscape' a painting by Olive Serres

Her husband John Serres was now officially Marine Painter to the King, an appointment that he had both 'inherited' from his late father Dominic and earned in his own right. This appointment brought him a great deal of profitable commissions, but nowhere near enough to satisfy the demands of Olive, whose extravagant lifestyle was way beyond both her own not insignificant earnings and the allowance he had provided for her when they separated. She took full advantage of the laws that allowed a married woman to pass liability for her debts to her husband, and John Serres was always in financial difficulties, being constantly pursued by her creditors, even to the point of being arrested and imprisoned for her unpaid bills. His desperation reached the point where, after one such arrest he issued a statement that:

This Bill is a forgery—my wife Olive Serres having drawn it and signed my name to it when I was on the coast of Spain on Government Service, and without my knowledge.

In 1807, when Mrs Serres was thirty-five, Dr Wilmot died. Six years later, in 1813, she published her memoir about him entitled *The Life of The Author of Junius' Letters, the Rev. James Wilmot DD,* which was where she first started making claims about Wilmot's Polish Princess; this memoir attracted attention however principally for its assertion that Wilmot was the author of *The Letters of Junius.* These anonymous *Letters* (there was no such person as 'Junius', this being merely a 'nom de plume') had been printed in *The Public Advertiser* between January 1769 and January 1772 as political commentaries and were clearly written by someone very familiar with the political scene of the time who was not afraid of making bold, provocative and sarcastic attacks on current events and personalities, even including the King. There had been considerable interest in identifying the anonymous author, and Mrs Serres, who was not unknown in London circles through her writings and paintings and her Royal connections, created a stir with this claim for authorship for her late uncle. The claim received a certain initial acceptance but was soon after dismissed in the light of an authoritative study of the letters and their handwriting in favour of the English politician Sir Philip Francis. She later published, in 1817, *Junius, Sir Philip Francis denied; a Letter addressed to the British Nation.* In support of her claim for

Wilmot's authorship, the 'Warwick' Archive in the Warwick Records office contains the following letter and note:

"Olive—

The Letters of Junius were my <u>Composition</u>. My friend Mr Dunning corrected the legal parts——Lord Chatham, S– and Lord Chesterfield patronized the Letters at the period of my labours to benefit my Country—but on 1773 His Majesty (the next few words are not legible) I resigned my pen for your sake Olive.   J.W."

Attached to this letter, and in the same hand, is the following note: "An exact copy of one of the Ps (Princess?) of Cumberlands papers <u>taken in 1824 </u>concerning Junius and Dr Wilmot"

The *Sir Philip Francis denied* title set a standard for much of her future literary output for she would, in pursuit of her ambitions, often publish florid and rambling *Letters* and *Appeals to the British Nation,* or, as in 1829 sometimes to *the English Nation* which was another statement of her case together with an appeal for funds, and on at least one occasion *to the Polish Nation.* The attached (Appendix 4) *Manifesto* to Poland is an example of her style.

The Public Records Office has a copy of Mrs Serres' 1813 book on Dr Wilmot. This particular copy has many textual annotations and corrections, which suggest that this may even have been her own copy being edited for a revised edition. In the page margins, and in a seemingly different script to these textual notes, are various comments such as, on page 28, 'Junius [ie Wilmot] united himself with a lady who was afterwards a Princess of Poland and everything was prepared for his residence in that Country when a fatal discovery compelled him to abandon his intentions.' And later, on page 116 Mrs Serres wrote: 'When the Princess of Poland visited England Dr Wilmot attended her to the University. She valued our author [Wilmot] exceedingly during her residence in England, and invited him to the Court of Poland; she frequently corresponded with him, after her departure from this kingdom.' The same hand as before has underlined the opening word 'When' and written a margin comment 'The second time that'. This latter annotation does at least support both the possibility that the Princess had visited England previously, when perhaps she first met Wilmot, and his undated 'diary' note in which he referred to (his wife) the Princess's visit in 1767, bringing wedding presents for his daughter, Olive Serres' mother.

Also in 1817, Mrs Serres petitioned King George III, for she was by now claiming recognition as the illegitimate daughter of Henry, Duke of Cumberland, by Dr Wilmot's sister Mrs Olive Payne. With the King in the final stages of his senility and within three years of death, Mrs Serres did not receive an acknowledgement but by the time he died, in January 1820, she had revised and renewed her claims. In a new petition, now to King George IV and dated December 1820, Mrs Serres had again revised her story; she was now Cumberland's *legitimate* daughter but from his *secret* marriage to Dr Wilmot's daughter; so she was now no longer Dr Wilmot's niece but his granddaughter. First she had thought she was his niece, being the daughter of his brother Robert; then she claimed to be still his niece, but this time because she was the illegitimate daughter of his sister Mrs Payne by a Royal Duke; finally she decided she was actually Wilmot's granddaughter, by virtue of being the daughter of his daughter, this same Royal Duke still being her father. And although Dr Wilmot had supposedly lived and died a bachelor, she maintained he had been secretly married to a Polish Princess. Further, said Mrs Serres, she had documents to prove each and every one of these revised claims. Dr Wilmot, according to this latest version, had a daughter Olive by his marriage, who had been given into the care of his sister Mrs Payne (the same lady who, in Mrs Serres' 1817 petition, was supposed to have been seduced by the Duke of Cumberland and given birth to a girl, also named Olive). The attractions of Dr Wilmot's Olive as a young woman, having charmed both the Earl of Warwick and the Duke of Cumberland, had resulted in her marriage to the Duke. The daughter of this marriage, also called Olive, later became Mrs Olive Serres. And again Mrs Serres was adamant about documentary proof of all of this. She was of course widely ridiculed, but she continued with this story, against all mockery, as certain of her proofs as she was of Dr Wilmot's alter ego *Junius*. She assumed the title of Princess of Cumberland, and later the additional title of Duchess of Lancaster because, she claimed, she had documents to prove the titles were hers (Appendix 1: No.17). Her answer to all questions of 'why wait till now to make these claims', when Dr Wilmot, who could have supported this preposterous story, was dead, was quite simply that she had known nothing of her origins until several years after Wilmot's death. This knowledge came to her, she said, with its associated proofs, from no less a person than the Earl of Warwick very shortly before *his* death, and was passed on to her by the Earl himself *in the presence of* Edward, Duke of Kent, a son of George III. Further, she had been particularly required by both Warwick and Kent not to disclose any of these matters until after the death of the King. Kent, she asserted, was very supportive of her claims, had acknowledged her as his cousin and had provided her with an annuity. Of course it didn't help her credibility in all this that both Warwick and Kent were also dead, Kent having died in the same week as his father.

Not making much progress with her claim for recognition as a 'royal' by virtue of being the daughter of the Duke of Cumberland, Mrs Serres revised her approach. She published a letter to the King (now George IV) stating her case that she was the Princess of Cumberland and formally requesting that this claim be carefully examined. This time she gained useful support from the Editor of a weekly journal, *The British Luminary*, he pointedly said that these were serious matters that demanded serious investigation and not just ridicule. Mrs Serres was, he said quite vigorously, entitled to the fair investigation she had requested; why should she not receive it? In 1821 she was introduced to Mr H N Bell, a leading young genealogist who had earned himself a considerable reputation for his successful prosecution of claims of disputed ancestry; he not only thought her claim was reasonable but undertook to act on her behalf, which for a while he did with seemingly good effect. But she was regarded as mad by *The Times*, and as an imposter by *The Morning Post*. Others commented merely that with the Hanovers you never knew who their children were, and that this sort of thing was what you got with German kings. But Mrs Serres persisted. She had herself re-baptised as *Olive, daughter of the Duke of Cumberland and Olive his wife*. But the Royal Court continued to ignore her.

Essentially, her story (final version) was that in 1815 the Earl of Warwick, a witness to the marital affairs of both George III and the Duke of Cumberland, became aware that he had not long to live. He contacted Edward, Duke of Kent, one of George III's sons, and told him all that he knew concerning Mrs Serres' and her origins. Edward (father of the future Queen Victoria), was immediately interested and together with Warwick called on Mrs Serres at her London home. There Warwick, in the presence of the Duke, and having extracted a pledge of secrecy from her until the death of George III, gave her the information concerning the circumstances of her birth. It was agreed that Warwick would return immediately to Warwick Castle to bring all the papers to London for the Duke to inspect (more than 100 of them) and he (Kent) signed as an indicator of authenticity those that were regarded as the most important. The papers were then handed over to Mrs Serres, together with two certificates to this effect signed by both Warwick and the Duke. (These two certificates form part of Mrs Serres' papers and still exist, see Appendix 1: Nos 20, 21).

Kent, Mrs Serres said, was so convinced of the authenticity of these papers that he promptly recognised her as his cousin (his Uncle Cumberland's daughter). He then made some arrangements for her financial security via Mr Robert Owen, the well-known and wealthy industrialist and social reformer with whom he had had many contacts, who would pay her an annuity of £400; and in a will left her some property, even stating his wish that she should be the guardian for his daughter. His belief in Mrs Serres is supposedly demonstrated in the following PRO document, written in 1819 just a few months before he died:

8. I solemnly testify my satisfaction at the proofs of Princess Olive of Cumberland's birth, and declare that my Royal parent's sign-manual to the certificates of my dearest cousin's birth are, to the best of my own comprehension and belief, the genuine handwriting of the King my father. Thus I constitute Olive, Princess of Cumberland, the guardian and director of my daughter Alexandrina's education from the age of four years and upwards, in the case of my death, and from the Duchess of Kent being so unacquainted with the mode of English education; and in case my wife departs this life in my daughter's minority, I constitute and appoint my cousin Olive the sole guardian of my daughter till she is of age. *['Alexandrina' was Alexandrina Victoria, later to become Queen Victoria].*

In January 1820 King George III and his son Edward, Duke of Kent died within a week of each other. Mrs Serres' pursuit of her rightful (as she saw it) status thus experienced a double jolt, for on the one hand she had lost a useful and powerful supporter, but on the other, with the King now dead there was no longer any requirement to withhold her claims. In an early step she publicly assumed the title of Princess of Cumberland, acquired a coach, and painted it and dressed her coachmen in appropriate Royal livery. In spite of the gossip that this inevitably inspired, she was not challenged by the Court and required to stop so she continued, inevitably giving rise to a public impression that her claims were valid. She was even invited, on Lord Mayor's Day in 1820 to the Lord Mayor's banquet where she was treated with the · deference and honour due to the rank she had assumed. The Dukes of Sussex and of Clarence (later King William IV), both sons of George III, took the opportunity, at different times and in different places, on all occasions with witnesses present, to inspect the documents. Both declared themselves satisfied as to the signatures of their father and their brother Edward. In spite of these however, petitions to King George IV supported by affidavits concerning the signatures to the various documents got nowhere.

Mrs Serres tried again, now with the following document from her portfolio (which is also in the Public Records Office) in an effort to obtain sight of the late King's Will:

9. George R.   St. James's
   In case of our Royal demise, we give and bequeath to Olive, our brother of Cumberland's daughter, the sum of £15,000, commanding our heir and successor to pay the same, privately, to our said niece, for her use, as a recompense for the misfortune she may have known through her father.
   June 2, 1774.
   Witness: J. Dunning. Chatham. Warwick.

First, Mrs Serres swore a lengthy affidavit as to the circumstances in which this (and other) documents came into her possession.

Second, two statements were sworn concerning the signature of the witness J. Dunning (a barrister). One was by a Mr Griffin, who stated that he entered the service of Mr Dunning in 1771 and continued with him until his death in 1781, and that during that time he became *'well-acquainted with his manner and character of handwriting and subscription'* and having examined this document he *'in his conscience believes the signature "J. Dunning" to be the proper handwriting and subscription of the said John Dunning.'* The second statement, in much the same terms, was sworn by a Thomas Lloyd who, as an attorney-at-law became *'well-acquainted... etc'* in the course of his work over many years with Mr Dunning (barrister), and similarly affirmed Dunning's signature.

Third, the matter of the King's own signature was examined. In May 1822 Mr John Vancouver (a brother of the famous Captain George Vancouver), swore that for seventeen years, until 1788/9, he was Deputy–Customer and Deputy-Collector at Lynn in Norfolk. In this capacity he had many opportunities of seeing the 'sign-manual' (signature) of the late King and thus became well acquainted with it. Having inspected the document presented to him he asserted, in the same style as before, that this had been signed by the King's own hand.

Fourth, this same Mr John Vancouver was for some sixteen years immediately preceding the death of the Earl of Warwick in 1816, intimately acquainted with the Earl, having correspondence with him and having seen him write and sign letters. He similarly swore that in his opinion the signature on the document shown to him was that of the Earl of Warwick. A second opinion on this was provided here, by a Mr John George, an auctioneer, who had transacted business for the Earl over many years; he also gave his opinion, in the same terms, that the Earl's signature was authentic. Finally, and interestingly, Mr John Dickenson swore in May 1822 that he was the only surviving executor of the late Earl; that he knew and was intimately acquainted with the Earl for about thirty years until his death and was perfectly well acquainted with...etc. and that he believed

...the whole body, series, and contents of the said paper, and every part of the same together with the date thereof—save only the name and letter 'George R', subscribed at the head thereto, and the letter and name 'J. Dunning' and the title 'Chatham', also subscribed as witnesses—to be all of the proper handwriting and subscription of the said George, Earl Brooke and Earl of Warwick, deceased.

In this affidavit we have Warwick's executor, who claimed under oath to have known him and to have been familiar with his handwriting for some thirty years, stating that this entire document other than the signatures, was actually written for the King not by some clerk or private Secretary, but by the Earl of Warwick himself, in his own hand.

Fifth, no living witness was found to attest to Chatham's signature.

This document, together with the affidavits supporting it, each properly sworn in the presence of a Notary Public and a witness, were in 1822 presented to the Courts in support of a request for probate of the King's will. However the four-day hearing did not even consider the authenticity or otherwise of the document but debated instead the technical problem of whether the Will of a sovereign could be probated. It appeared that the only Royal Will ever to have been deposited in the Court was that of Henry VIII 300 years previously, and that wasn't the original but simply a copy. The Court concluded that a Royal Will couldn't be probated at all, so in spite of Mrs Serres' efforts, the Legacy and its supporting documents, the notarised witness statements, were not examined and again nothing was achieved. Later in that year she again applied for permission to view King George's final Will, but again the Court found that it had no jurisdiction.

She tried once more, now using the less costly Doctors' Commons procedures, but still without a result. [The *College of Advocates and Doctors of Law*, familiarly known as 'Doctors Commons', had been founded in 1511. To be admitted as a Fellow of the College one had to have attained the degree of Doctor of Civil Law from either Oxford or Cambridge University. Fellows shared facilities, such as a common dining/meeting hall, clerks and a common writing room. The College was near St. Paul's where the Ecclesiastical Courts were formerly held, and wills were preserved there. A certain amount of Admiralty work was also dealt with there. To 'common' meant to dine together, a term still used at universities today, and it was a requirement that Fellows had to dine together for four days in each term, a custom known as 'eating their term'. The College was closed in 1859 following the establishment of the Court of Probate, and the buildings demolished as part of an extensive redevelopment of the area'}

A supporter, Sir Gerard Noel MP, agreed to present a petition in the House of Commons on Mrs Serres' behalf for an official enquiry into her case. But she was unfortunate in her man for Sir Gerard was an ineffectual person whose motion was easily despatched by the Home Secretary Mr (later, Sir) Robert Peel. He dealt with the matter of the King's Will by simply arguing that Chatham had resigned Office in 1768 and had said later that he had had no access to the King until 1775. Mr Peel interpreted this to mean that in 1774 the King was not even on good terms with Lord Chatham so that it was unlikely that he would have asked Chatham to witness such a private matter. Other witness signatures were similarly brushed aside. The matter of the signature of 'Addez' on the marriage certificate of Cumberland to Olive Wilmot (Appendix 1: No 8) was mockingly disposed of by referring to it as 'Adder' and then suggesting that this was supposed to have been someone named 'Hadow' but some uneducated person had presumably dropped an 'aitch'. (This debate in The House of Commons was later referred to in the 1866 trial by the Lord Chief Justice.) The petition failed: Sir Gerard succumbed to Mr Peel's brusque treatment and did not even press for a division, so no official enquiry would be set up.

By now Mrs Serres was in serious financial trouble. She had indulged in extravagant expenditure in adopting the style of Princess of Cumberland, and she had incurred heavy legal costs in pursuing her claims. Also, her income had dried up. Her support from the Duke of Kent had ceased with his death, and her allowance from her husband was not being regularly paid as he too was suffering from the same financial problems created by his wife's extravagances. She was arrested on a promissory note that had not been met. She entered bail and, seizing her opportunity, pleaded that as a member of the Royal Family she was privileged from arrest as in this way, and by pure chance, this arrest offered her an opportunity to argue in Court her case for recognition as a 'royal'. It turned out however that because she had perfected bail she was not eligible to plead privilege; the opportunity was lost, and she was committed to jail until her debt was repaid. This she achieved principally by her writings; she published a series of astronomical studies, and announced her invention of separate North and South compasses designed to compensate for the different navigation problems which, she had determined, were to be found on opposite sides of the equator. She was released in 1827, re-arrested in 1828 and again released, having spent the best part of six years in prison. Interestingly, her committal into and release from prison were both in the name of the Princess of Cumberland. In 1834, aged 62, she died, financially ruined and deeply disappointed. She was buried in St. James's, Piccadilly, as Princess of Cumberland by sanction of the Home Secretary.

She had many times asked for her claims and her documents to be examined, but each time her requests were either ignored or evaded, as with her attempt to get Probate for King George's Will, or when she was arrested for debt and pleaded privilege, a plea which was sidestepped rather than examined.

But also she had given ridiculously inconsistent stories concerning her supposed origins, and much of the mass of documentation in support of her claim to membership of the Royal family was regarded as suspect for content, style, and in terms of how she came by them. For example she claimed to have been made aware of her 'true' origins, ie as the granddaughter of Dr Wilmot, in 1815; yet in 1817, in her *Sir Philip Francis Denied* publication, she stated that Dr Wilmot had never married; and then in 1821 she said he had married a sister of King Stanislaus of Poland; in 1819, in her *Letters from the Earl of Warwick to Mrs Serres* she referred to herself as Dr Wilmot's niece; ten years later, in 1829, she was his granddaughter again in her *Address to the English Nation*. She claimed to have received most of her documents directly from the Earl of Warwick, in the presence of the Duke of Kent; yet she wrote a letter describing in graphic terms how an additional 'paquet' of these documents had afterwards been hand-delivered to her when she answered a knock at her front door to be confronted by the ghost of the then late Earl of Warwick with this 'paquet' in its outstretched hand. This additional 'delivery' story had seemingly been necessary in order to explain why she hadn't known about, amongst other things, Dr Wilmot's supposed marriage. Hardly surprisingly, accusations of fraud and forgery came to haunt her even more than Warwick's ghost.

In addition to her considerable talents in writing and in painting she was by all accounts, like her mother before her, a very attractive woman of great charm and good conversation. She had two daughters, Lavinia and Britannia, by her husband, though in his Will John Serres accused his wife of having had several lovers and having had children by them which she gave away (this particular accusation has not been supported or repeated by anyone else). She was totally single-minded about her campaign for recognition, capable of quite ruthless steps if they might move her nearer to her objective. She worked hard with her writing (particularly) and painting to earn money for this campaign yet continually spent far more than she earned in both financing it and in extravagant living. Apart from her paintings and her own publications of books and *English Nation* addresses and the like, her name is also associated with authorship of the anonymous *Authentic Records of the Court of England* published in 1831, and with Lady Anne Hamilton's *Secret History of the Court of England;* these two books are virtually the same, as even their titles suggest. Both contain pages relevant to matters here, with much the same form of words in both. However virtually nothing in either work is substantiated, much is recognisably gossip, and they are widely condemned with the single word 'scandalous'. Lady Hamilton, who was a Lady in Waiting to Princess (later Queen) Caroline, and was the sister of the Duke of Hamilton, always denied authorship of *Secret History* yet she took no steps to have her name and picture removed. Mrs Serres, who had long been acquainted with Lady Hamilton (one of the poems in her 1805 publication *Flights of Fancy* is entitled 'To Lady Hamilton'), was often thought to have been, if not the author, then at least her collaborator. However there is no proof of Mrs Serres' authorship. In her Will, Olive Serres had her final word concerning her claims. It contains the following clause:

I bequeath to all my cousins of the Royal House of Guelph the sum of one shilling to each, to enable them to purchase a prayer for to teach them repentance for their past cruelties and injuries to myself, their legitimate and lawful cousin.

But her fight continued through her daughter, Mrs Lavinia Ryves, also now styling herself Princess of Cumberland and Duchess of Lancaster. In 1844 she enlisted again the help of Sir Gerard Noel and a small group of financial supporters and in 1846 they filed a Bill against the Duke of Wellington, as executor of King George IV (successor to George III), for an account of the legacy of £15,000, which had not been paid. And again the Court refused to help, for it said that it had no powers concerning a Will that had not been proved (ie probated).

The Lavinia Ryves Trial

Mrs Lavinia Ryves

Mrs Serres having died, it was exclusively her elder daughter Lavinia Ryves who was a family supporter of her royalist claims. Robert Wilmot, who had raised Olive in her earliest years as his daughter, had always denied her claims, pointing out that he had signed, as her *father*, the authority for her to marry Mr Serres. (Mrs Serres dealt with that by arguing that he was simply being true to an oath he had sworn to his brother to keep the secret of her birth). John Serres had also made it clear he did not believe these stories, and their younger daughter Brittannia, having been in the care of her father, shared his view. Lavinia had married Anthony Thomas Ryves, a portrait painter, and become the mother of six children so she was in no position to help her own mother in her final years, nor even, following her mother's death, to pursue the case herself since Mr Ryves had run off with their maid and left his wife with the care and responsibility of their children. But in 1841, by which time she had divorced her husband and her children were grown, she was ready to return to the fray.

The tide of opinion on the matter was starting to turn and in 1848, over a period from May to September *The Morning Post* (later incorporated into *The Daily Telegraph)*, the same journal that some twenty years earlier had called her mother an imposter, published a series of articles investigating and analysing Mrs Ryves' claims and, more importantly, the documents that formed their basis. This newspaper now claimed in these articles that it had subjected these documents to rigorous investigation:

.....If we can show, as we believe we shall be able to do, that there does exist, at this moment and in this Country, a case of grievous and flagrant wrong;...

The *Morning Post* stated in these articles that in 1822 Mrs Serres had found people then still living who provided written testament that they recognised as genuine certain of the signatures, including those of Dr Wilmot and the Duke of Kent. Among its various conclusions it said:

That man must be a more than intrepid infidel who, in the face of documents as these will venture to disbelieve that the Duke of Cumberland was lawfully married to Miss Wilmot on the 4th March, 1767. It is equally a fact that, on the 2nd of Oct, 1771, his Royal Highness, his first wife being then alive, did contract a marriage with Lady Anne Horton....

It is unfortunate that *The Morning Post* was not a little more rigorous with its own editing; these articles introduced errors that did Mrs Ryves' case no good whatsoever, for she incorporated the articles verbatim into her later *Appeal for Royalty* which became part of the evidence in the trial. For instance, the *Post* stated that Dr Wilmot had married Stanislaus' *daughter*, though both Olive Serres and Dr Wilmot had said that it was his sister. This further undermined any belief in Mrs Serres' (and thus her daughter Mrs Ryves') already very suspect ability to tell a consistent story. The *Post* also stated that Hannah Lightfoot's will was dated 1768, whereas the date was 1762; and that Dr Wilmot's doctorate was awarded in 1766 (the actual date was 1760). This gave rise to accusations that Mrs Serres had not merely forged the Will but had carelessly given it a date that would of itself prove the forgery.

In March 1850 Mrs Ryves sent a letter to the Queen referring to her 'connection' to Her Majesty and attaching a 'Memorial', which summarised her claims; this ended on the note

That your Memorialist is reduced to the greatest state of poverty and distress, and with six children entirely dependent on her, she feels compelled to make her case generally known, in the hope that a generous Public will afford her such pecuniary assistance as is necessary, not only for her present actual subsistence, but also for the further prosecution of those claims to which she feels justly entitled, and of which she is so cruelly and wrongfully deprived.

This claim about having 'six children entirely dependent on her' was quite silly since she was by then aged fifty three and her children were all adults. However the prompt reply from Buckingham Palace, dated March 14th 1850, read:

I have received the commands of Her Majesty the Queen, to inform you, in reply to your application, dated yesterday, that the claims advanced in that letter render it impossible for Her Majesty to accede to your request for pecuniary assistance.

The speed and content of this response made the Queen's attitude quite clear. Mrs Ryves then published as a pamphlet *An Appeal for Royalty: being a letter to Her Majesty the Queen* which incorporated the full text of the articles (complete with errors) in the *Post*, but also with copies of many of the certificates and attestations added. At the end of it there came both a threat and a demand. The *threat* was that she would publish documents 'proving' the marriage of George III to Hannah Lightfoot. Although rumour and gossip had ensured that this story was widely known, these particular papers had never been published. Now however, more than thirty years after George's death, Mrs Ryves declared her readiness to expose the whole story if she didn't receive what she regarded as her right and for which her mother had fought for so long. Her *demand* was for compensation from the Queen personally: she wanted first, £846,016, which was the estimated monetary value of arrears of rents and profits due to the Duchy of Lancaster; second, the £15,000 due under George III's will; and third, the payment of legacies which she claimed were left to her mother by the Duke of Kent, the Queen's father (for which supporting documents are included in the PRO file on the case). Against the public revenue of the Country she made no claims, not wishing 'to take a single penny from my heavily-burdened and over-taxed fellow-countrymen as the price of the injustice done by their rulers.'

There was no response. So, taking advantage in 1861 of the new Legitimacy Declaration Act of 1858, Mrs Ryves first set out to establish her own legitimacy, under the terms of this Act, as the 'lawful daughter of John Thomas Serres and Olive his wife'. With this declaration under her belt, she then set out to establish the legality of her grandmother's marriage to the Duke of Cumberland. This was the next step to then proving her right, having been confirmed as her mother's legitimate daughter, to claiming George III's still unpaid legacy of £15,000. The claim was heard in the Divorce and Matrimonial Courts, in June 1866.

The case had both major constitutional significance and a serious financial aspect to it, quite apart from Mrs Ryves's intent on establishing her royal status. For the Crown was now well aware of the nature of the documentary evidence to be presented, and anyway Mrs Ryves' *Appeal to Royalty* earlier had demonstrated that if she won there would financial claims to follow in the order of £1million. This was not a case that the Crown could even consider losing. The hearing was before the Lord Chief Justice, the Lord Chief Baron and the Judge Ordinary. The Attorney General represented himself since he was notionally the respondent to the appeal, and he had the Solicitor General and two QC's in support; a Special Jury had been empanelled. Mrs Ryves, with her very limited resources simply could not afford to hire matching legal firepower and was represented only by a junior barrister, Dr J W Smith, and his assistant.

The Lord Chief Justice first pointed out to her that, whatever the outcome of this trial, she could never inherit the legacy (assuming also that she were able to prove that there was one) because, even if she proved her mother's legitimacy as the daughter of the Duke of Cumberland, the marriage to Mr Serres had not been authorised under the Royal Marriages Act, so that she (Mrs Ryves) could not be her mother's *legitimate* heir in this matter; nevertheless the trial went ahead. (This was a very harsh approach to the case, which set the tone for the rest of it; for even assuming that the legitimacy were established, Mrs Serres would clearly not have asked for Royal permission to marry since at that time she would simply have had no idea that it could be necessary.) After some preliminary argument, Mrs Ryves' Counsel, Dr Smith, opened his case, presenting a number of documents, including those that showed the marriage of the Prince of Wales to Hannah Lightfoot:

Two certificates (available at the PRO at Kew) (Appendix 1: No 7,8) testify to the marriage of the Duke of Cumberland and Olive Wilmot:

10. The marriage of the underwritten parties was duly solemnised, according to the rites and ceremonies of the Church of England, at Thomas Lord Archers' house, London, March the 4th, 1767, by myself.

J. Wilmot
Henry Frederick
Olive Wilmot

Present at the marriage of these parties: Brooke

Attested before:
J. Addez
J. Dunning .
Chatham

11. I solemnly certify that I married Henry Frederick Duke of Cumberland to Olive Wilmot, March the fourth, 1767, and that such marriage was lawfully solemnised at Thomas Lord Archer's house (at nine in the evening), in Grosvenor Square, London.

J. Wilmot

Witness to this marriage: Brooke

J. Addez

Attested before: Chatham

J. Dunning

These are potentially much more significant than it would appear because, *endorsed on the back of these two documents* are the following, relating to the George/Hannah marriage:

12. This is to solemnly certify, that I married George Prince of Wales to Princess Hannah, his first consort, April 17, 1759, and that two princes and a princess were the issue of such marriage.
London, April 2, 1760   J. Wilmot.

13. This is to certify to all it may concern, that I lawfully married George Prince of Wales to Hannah Lightfoot, April 17, 1759, and that two sons and a daughter are the issue of such marriage.

J. Wilmot
Chatham
J. Dunning

The Bench (and the Attorney General) then commented as follows:

The Lord Chief Baron. 'We are bound to take notice that George III was publicly married to Queen Charlotte, and that they were publicly crowned. If there was a prior marriage, and the first wife was living at the time of the second marriage, George IV may have had no right to the throne.'

The Attorney General. 'Nor her present Majesty. I do not disguise from myself that this is nothing less than a claim to the throne.'

The Lord Chief Justice. 'In my opinion it is indecent to go on with an inquiry into such matters unless it is absolutely necessary for the purposes of justice.'

The Attorney General: 'I am bound to tell your Lordships that I shall treat it as a case of fraud, fabrication and imposture from beginning to end. It is comfortable to believe that the guilt of the fraud may be excused or palliated by the insanity of one of the persons principally concerned.'

The Attorney General may, indeed, have been right about 'her present Majesty', but there was absolutely nothing about the case that either implied or suggested that anyone, least of all Mrs Ryves, was trying to claim the throne.

There followed presentation of a great many documents, and evidence in support of the signatures—necessary since every one of the signatories was now dead—given by Mr Frederick Netherclift, the foremost handwriting expert of the day. There were robust challenges to his opinions by the Attorney General, which forced him to modify certain of them but he remained firm on his view that the signatures were genuine.

Dr Smith proposed to question Mrs Ryves as to the declaration made by Hannah Lightfoot, wife of George III.

The Lord Chief Justice: 'At present we have no evidence of the marriage of George III to Hannah Lightfoot.' Counsel then referred to the two documents certifying the marriage.

The Lord Chief Justice: 'The Court is as I understand, asked solemnly to declare on the strength of two certificates, coming I know not whence, written on two scraps of paper, that the marriage, the only marriage of George III which the world believes to have taken place, between His Majesty and Queen Charlotte, was an invalid marriage, and consequently that all the Sovereigns who have sat upon the throne since his death, including her present Majesty, were not entitled to sit upon the throne. That is the conclusion, which the Court is asked to come to upon these two rubbishy pieces of paper, one signed George P., and the other George Guelph (the family name of the Hanovers). I believe them to be gross and rank forgeries. The Court has no difficulty in coming to the conclusion, even assuming the signatures had that character of genuineness which they have not, that what is asserted in these documents has not the slightest foundation in fact.'

The Lord Chief Baron: 'I wish to express my entire concurrence in the opinion of the Lord Chief Justice, and I think that the declarations of Hannah Lightfoot, if there ever was such a person, cannot be received in evidence on the faith of these documents.'

The Judge Ordinary: 'The Court is entirely unanimous on this question. My own opinion, formed not only on the evidence I have heard, but also the evidence of my own eyes, is that these documents are nothing more nor less than very foolish forgeries. I am not at all sorry that the occasion has arisen for bringing them into a Court of Justice, where their authenticity can be enquired into by evidence, for the existence of documents of this sort is calculated to set abroad a number of idle stories, for which there is probably not the slightest foundation.'

The Lord Chief Justice: 'I have another reason for attaching no value whatever to these documents. It is my profound conviction, resulting from the most careful and deliberate attention I can give to the question, that the signatures "J. Wilmot" are also forgeries.'

The evidence as to Hannah Lightfoot was accordingly excluded.

These signatures of Dr Wilmot had already been declared genuine by Mr Netherclift, particularly those certifying the marriage of George to Hannah, where he further attested that the *writing* of the certificates was also that of Dr Wilmot. He had been strongly challenged, and admitted that he had not seen an original signature of Wilmot's and that this opinion was based on tracings which he understood to be genuine. He was then presented with genuine original signatures of Dr Wilmot taken from the registers of Barton-on-the-Heath and from Trinity College. He said again that, comparing the signatures on the Court documents against those now presented to him, they were genuine. Challenged over the fact that many times the same person's signature on many documents was not always the same, Netherclift stated that that strengthened his opinions since signatures were not always consistent and did in any event change over the years. Had they always been the same, this would have been a cause to doubt their authenticity. These Wilmot signatures had also been supported by a lot of other evidence. Netherclift was similarly firm and positive concerning King George's signatures. But the Lord Chief Justice was determined that these signatures, particularly the Wilmot ones, were forgeries.

In his opening statement for the Crown the Attorney General had referred to a letter from Mrs Serres' former Counsel, Mr Bell, identifying another whole family of documents besides those produced. One of these, he said, supposedly certified the remarriage of George III to Queen Charlotte after the death of 'Queen' Hannah; another stated that William, Duke of Clarence was the King's legitimate son, ie born after this re-marriage. None of these were presented at the trial.

Before calling Mrs Ryves to the Witness Box, Dr Smith observed that almost up to her death in 1834, Mrs Serres had made every effort to have her case examined by a competent Court.
The Lord Chief Baron: 'You cannot be ignorant that there was a debate in The House of Commons several years ago, in which they were denounced as forgeries by the late Sir Robert Peel.'
Dr Smith: 'Sir Robert talked great nonsense in that speech.'

Mrs Ryves was not helped by the early contradictory and confusing claims made by her mother; nor by some of the evidence she herself gave concerning her mother. The

Attorney General did not hesitate to score easy points: he asked about a spelling mistake in the 1821 letter to George IV ('offspring' spelt as 'orfspring') and when Mrs Ryves said that that mistake must have been made by Mr Bell he produced a 'Congratulatory Ode' written by Mrs Serres in 1812 in honour of the Prince Regent's birthday, which showed the same spelling error. Mrs Ryves was not put off: she responded that she was over 70 and could not always remember all the details of past events "although I am here with a good will and spirit, it is a task to go backwards and forwards in a hurry". She later gave the Attorney General another easy point when, asked if her mother believed in ghosts, she replied that she did not, yet then identified a letter as having been written by her mother which vividly described a confrontation on her own doorstep with the ghost of the dead Lord Warwick.

The Attorney General gave a very well regarded closing address to the Jury, describing the documents in the case as

the most ridiculous, absurd, preposterous series of forgeries that the perverted ingenuity of man ever invented. Not only were they not produced until every person whose signatures appeared on them was safely dead, but they were all written on scraps and slips of paper, without watermarks, which no human being would ever have used for the purpose of recording transactions of this kind.

At this point the Foreman of the Jury interrupted him to say that they, the Jury, didn't feel the need to hear anything more as they were all agreed that the documents were not genuine.

The Lord Chief Justice: 'You share the opinion which my learned brothers and I have entertained for a long time, that every one of the documents is spurious.'

Mrs Ryves' Counsel insisted on his right to address the Jury.

The Lord Chief Justice: 'If you wish to take up any more of their time you have a right to do so.'

Dr Smith (to the Jury): 'I believe on my word of honour as a gentleman that the documents that the petitioner [Mrs. Ryves] had produced—'

The Lord Chief Justice: 'I insist on your not finishing that sentence. It is a violation of a fundamental rule of conduct, which every advocate ought to observe, to give the jury your personal opinion.'

Dr Smith then went on to note that the trial had been prejudiced from the outset by the inaccurate statement of the Attorney General that it was a claim by his client upon the throne. Next, refuting the Attorney General's comments concerning the character of Mrs Serres, he asked rhetorically: "Is it not a fact that she received an allowance of £400 a year from the Duke of Kent" "It is a perfect fiction", interrupted the Attorney General. Yet he knew, as he also knew that Dr Smith could not have known, that this allowance which had been paid by Mr Robert Owen on behalf of the Duke,(Appendix 1: Nos 24,25,26), had been refunded in 1859 to Mr Owen's son by Kent's daughter, Queen Victoria herself.

The Duke of Kent had died before he had the opportunity to repay this money to Mr Owen, who was wealthy enough not to request repayment. But years later, in February 1859 his son Robert Dale Owen, the Scottish-American social reformer, who had been reviewing his late father's papers, found documents showing that the late Duke of Kent had owed some £1,200 to his late father for financial assistance to Mrs. Serres. (An additional source for the 'discovery' of these documents is in the Documents Appendix, No. 26). He sent these to the Queen requesting repayment; on 8th March 1859 he received a reply from a Mr Phipps advising that:

It would be very disagreeable to her Majesty to think any gentleman should have suffered in pecuniary affairs...because of the character of your father, and as you are obviously a gentleman...she considers it would not be advantageous to enter into any examination of the details of the different sums. It would be more agreeable to the Queen to fix at once the largest sum, ie £1,200. [*Princess Olive*, Margaret Shepard]

Mr Phipps added that the letters "would be better detained here" and therefore be no longer available to the Owen family as evidence. On 11ᵗʰ March, Mr. Owen signed a receipt for the money.

Counsel's address to the Jury was further interrupted both by the Lord Chief Justice and the Attorney General, even though opening and closing speeches are supposed to be free from interruption. After the Jury formally stated that they were not satisfied as to the documents in the case, the Attorney General then said that he had been quite prepared to prove that Dr Wilmot could not possibly have married his daughter to the Duke of Cumberland since he was in residence in Oxford on the day of the supposed marriage and did not come 'out of residence' until the next day. Yet even in the eighteenth century (as was observed by *The Morning Post* in its 1848 articles) it was quite possible to be in Oxford in the day, in London the same evening—one of the marriage certificates explicitly states that the marriage took place 'at nine in the evening'—and be back in Oxford the following morning. The late evening time of the proceedings was clearly arranged especially to permit Dr Wilmot to fulfil his commitments in Oxford and then to be in London in order to officiate at his daughter's marriage.

It is difficult to read the report of the Ryves trial without feeling that the Court was determined from the outset that she wouldn't win. Aside from the many weaknesses and contradictions built into Mrs Ryves' evidence, virtually all of them created by her mother Mrs Serres, which the Lord Chief Justice and the Attorney General very clearly exposed, the Court environment was totally hostile to her, and the Lord Chief Justice himself was the determinant of that. And his conduct of the case, with his critical comments and interruptions on the nature of the evidence, does not come across as that to be expected of a Judge sitting with a Jury, least of all the country's most senior Judge.

Almost 100 years ago, in her book *The Fair Quaker* published in 1910, Mary Pendered had a similar view:

It is in fact perfectly clear that, from the first, and before expert evidence as to the authenticity of the signatures had been called, the Court had made up its mind to reject Mrs

Ryves' case with contempt and contumely. Her sanity was called into question, she was even called insane.

Mrs Ryves was after what she saw as justice for herself. She lost it not because of the weaknesses in her case, which were real enough, but because the Court was focussed on something else, the Lightfoot marriage, that was actually irrelevant to her but of such overriding constitutional significance that her case had to be crushed. On the final motion of the Attorney General, the Court ordered all the documents produced as evidence to be impounded, and one has to wonder why. After all they were just 'gross and rank forgeries' on 'rubbishy pieces of paper'; why not simply return them to Mrs Ryves? Or have them destroyed? Why order them to be hidden away? And why, after having done 'nothing less than (laid) a claim to the throne' by means of these 'foolish' forgeries was Mrs Ryves not prosecuted with the full force of the law? After all there wouldn't have been much difficulty, in the circumstances, in mounting and proving a charge of treason. Informed opinion at the time seems to have been that the production of these documents had caused consternation, which was reason enough no doubt to 'rubbish' them, even though general opinion seems to have been that they were genuine. (In 1847, Mrs Clissold, who was the daughter of the then Lord Chief Justice Sir John Bayley, and who had been acquainted with Mrs Ryves since 1837, wrote that '...my father frequently observed to me he had no doubt of her [Mrs. Serres] claim being a just demand...'). Probably, prosecuting Mrs Ryves would have simply disinterred a matter, which had just been so satisfactorily buried.

Mrs Ryves however was not prepared to give up the fight. She arranged for another pamphlet to be published entitled *Was Justice Done?* and lodged an immediate appeal to the House of Lords. This appeal, which took two years before it was heard on 22nd June 1868, was very brief. It was dismissed within minutes on the technical grounds that no bill of exceptions had been entered, and that no motion for a new trial had been made, so their Lordships were unable to hear the claimant. (One wonders why Mrs Ryves' advisers were not informed beforehand by the Court officials of these deficiencies.) She tried again, entering a new appeal. Nothing was achieved however, for on 7th December 1871 she died before this renewed appeal to the Lords could be heard, and her case died with her.

Her mother had made many attempts over many years to obtain a judicial hearing of her claims; Mrs Ryves had had to wait more years for a date for her 1866 trial, a further two years just for her few brief minutes in The House of Lords, and had been waiting 3½ more years for her next appointment with justice when she died. As she herself asked: was justice done?

There had been considerable overseas interest in the trial and, not surprisingly given that it was George III who had presided over the loss of the American Colonies, particularly from America whose newspapers sent over representatives to cover the trial. Mrs Ryves had unsuccessfully tried to introduce her mother's portrait, together with selected portraits of the Royal family, as evidence, on the grounds that her alleged similarity to them would support her case. The American Law Review of 1867 reported:

The picture of Mrs Serres was not allowed to be shown in Court. It was shown in the lunch-room, and bore a remarkable resemblance to the portraits of George IV and William IV. The Attorney General, on returning, anxiously asked if the Jury had seen it and, being told they had not, ordered it to be carefully covered up.

In her publication *George Greville, Earl of Brooke and Warwick, Letters and Poems to Mrs Wilmot Serres* a letter (undated, but headed 'Six o'Clock, Evening) reads:

'Dear Mrs S., I write in haste but I must give you an account of the reception I had; a most courteous one, and I never like the P— R— [Prince Regent, later George IV] better. He reminded me so greatly of yourself: his eyes are very like yours; he smiles as you do, and, all considering, that His Royal Highness is light complexioned and you yourself a brunette, yet there is, certainly, an amazing resemblance!....'

Mrs Serres, never one to miss an opportunity, had also exploited this resemblance. In her Address to the English Nation of 1829, which was an appeal for funds to help her continue her campaign, she referred to her first encounter with the Duke of Kent when, she said, "he was so struck with my strong resemblance to the family that he saluted me as his cousin".

The following story was told by Mrs Ryves during her examination in the trial. It was not discussed since it was clearly unprovable, but whether true or not it throws an interesting light on the case according to the way in which it is considered.

In September 1820 Mrs Serres' Counsel, Mr Bell, who had been in ongoing discussions with Palace officials, arrived at her home greatly excited. He had been informed that King George IV had issued instructions that she was to be officially recognised as the Duchess of Cumberland and that all measures necessary for her comfort in this status were to be put in place. But within a day or two he (Mr Bell) had begun to back off very sharply from any further involvement in her case, and then resigned any further responsibility for it. The promised Royal decree and measures never materialised. It was another major disappointment for Mrs Serres but one, which in the circumstances seemed so pointless. It was some years later before an explanation surfaced. Mr Bell's ailing widow, wanting to put matters straight, called on Mrs Serres and explained that Mr Bell had suddenly stopped all his efforts on her behalf because he had been well paid to do so by the King's then heir, his brother Frederick, Duke of York. George IV had no surviving children so York, who was the next in line of succession to the throne ahead of their younger brother William, was anxious to avoid any possible damage to himself and his own probable succession from these intended moves by the King. The damage clearly would have been that if the King's intentions were completed he (York) like his elder brother George could have been declared illegitimate since he too was born before his parent's re-marriage, and thus not be able to succeed him as the next Monarch.

There is some substance to the basic point concerning the King's decision to recognise Mrs Serres. Included in the *Letters of King George IV* is a letter dated simply 'Wednesday, September 1820', from Sir William Gell, to William Vizard (a famous explorer of the day, Gell's interest at Court is not clear; Vizard was a prominent lawyer who was involved for the defence in the case against Queen Caroline) which has

....Her Highness the Duchess of Cumberland, alias Mrs Serres, who *will be acknowledged as I know* in a few days......(The italics are in the original).

If the story is true, the alleged bribe was sufficient for the purpose, although York himself did not profit from it since he died, childless, before George, leaving the succession to their next brother, William. Mrs Bell also supposedly said that Mr Bell too died not long after taking the bribe, without having had much opportunity to enjoy his extra wealth. Mr Bell did actually die in October 1822, at the early age of thirty, which would indeed have given him only a little time to spend this money. However at the time of his death he seems to have been under some pressure. Although he had recently received £5,000 to take on another case, he was also being sued by a creditor; and he seems to have spent a lot of time (and money?) on Mrs Serres' affairs even though she would probably not have been paying him. Presumably his fees from her would come after he had won her case. He lost the matter over which he was being sued, died that same evening, and was subsequently declared to have been insolvent at the time. After the trial Mrs Ryves claimed to have obtained further evidence concerning this story, to the effect that Mr Bell had been spending very heavily shortly before he died, evidence which would have been presented in her appeal.

Hannah *Regina*

Mrs Hannah Axford, née Lightfoot

The 1866 trial *Ryves v. the Attorney General* was demonstrably nothing more than a cover-up by denial of George III's early marriage to Hannah Lightfoot. This marriage had taken place, it was legal, she was therefore in truth Queen Hannah and in consequence, his subsequent marriage to Princess Charlotte was illegal and his successor, his eldest son by Charlotte, George Prince of Wales (George IV), had no right to the throne. As a by-product, there had also been a huge miscarriage of justice for Mrs Serres and her descendants. There are three threads to this argument: (i) Queen Charlotte's re-marriage (ii) the question of the validity, or invalidity, of the documents presented at the Ryves trial and (iii) the conduct of this trial itself, the Attorney

General's deceit, and the confiscation and concealment of the trial documents.

The Royal re-marriage: Rumours about the Hannah Lightfoot marriage were so persistent in the early years of King George's reign that, according to yet more rumours, Queen Charlotte insisted upon a second marriage ceremony, to which the King agreed. This is always said to have occurred in the summer of 1765, under cover of an entertainment at Kew Palace, with the marriage being performed by Dr Wilmot. The existence of a supposed certificate of this re-marriage was referred to by the Attorney General in his opening statement in the trial, though it was never produced. But any re-marriage taking place for reason of Hannah Lightfoot would be completely pointless unless there had been proof that she was dead. There is a document in the Public Records Office collection in Kew, also signed by Dr Wilmot, which refers to Hannah having died on December 1st 17?4, the third digit being unreadable (Appendix 1: No 4). Although this document itself is undated, the dates within it indicate it must have been written sometime during or after 1772. Taken together with the summer 1765 story, these indicate that Hannah died in December 1764 when she would have just passed her 34th birthday, since it is reasonable to expect that Charlotte would have wished to legitimise her marriage and her future children as soon after as possible. A 1754 date is not possible, since Hannah didn't marry the Prince of Wales until 1759 and anyway was still living in 1762 when she made her Will. And of course a re-marriage in 1765 (or later) would have been completely pointless unless the King *had* married Hannah *and* that definite news had been received of her death; this would rule out all the later decades, eg 1774, 1784, etc. No certificate of the re-marriage has ever been produced although, as said, there was reference to it by the Attorney General in his opening statement. Assuming the event happened, production of the certificate would of course immeasurably strengthen the general view at the time that their original marriage was invalid (why else would there be a re-marriage?); not being available does not alter the strength of the rest of the argument. However there is more to this re-marriage story than just rumours about rumours:

During the Ryves trial there were exchanges between the Lord Chief Justice and Dr Smith concerning the signature 'Chatham' on some of the documents. 'Chatham' of course was the same person who signed himself as 'Pitt' or 'W. Pitt' before he became Earl of Chatham in July 1766, from which date he would have used 'Chatham' for signing or witnessing documents. The Lord Chief Justice used this point to challenge the validity of documents supposedly bearing the signature 'Chatham' which had a date prior to July 1766; a fair point indeed. Yet all of these cases involved 3rd party references, such as for instance when Mr Bell (Mrs Serres' former Counsel) was quoted as referring to a 1765 document which he had said was witnessed by 'Chatham'. That document had to be a forgery, said the Lord Chief Justice, and went on:

"I have seen another letter which certifies that His Majesty was married to Queen Charlotte after the death of Queen Hannah in January 1765 by Dr Moore and this is certified by J Dunning and Chatham" [This could possibly have been the document referred to by the Attorney General at the outset of the Ryves trial).

The clear point here is that with 'Chatham' as a signature on a 1765 document it too had to have been a forgery. Dr Smith's response was that this was simply a mode of speech since Pitt was always, after his ennoblement, referred to as 'Chatham' so even if this letter had in fact been signed by *'Pitt'* his signature would later have been referred to, 'as a mode of speech', as that of *'Chatham'*. Of course the Lord Chief Justice did not say he had seen this marriage certificate, only the letter (of unknown date and origin) which certified it. But even although the letter was never produced, this clear statement of its existence by no less a person than the Lord Chief Justice is sufficient proof that it existed and could have been made available. One asks: why, having referred to it, was it not introduced as evidence for examination? The Lord Chief Justice named neither the sender nor the recipient of this letter, and there was no other challenge from the Court to its validity following Dr Smith's rebuttal of the original criticism. Could the sender and recipient have themselves, whoever they were, simply have been beyond criticism in this respect? The letter apparently did not state that the re-marriage had taken place but 'certified' it (the Lord Chief Justice's word); and the Dr Moore who is 'certified' to have carried it out proves to be Dr John Moore, at the time a Canon of Christ Church, Oxford who later went on to become, in 1783, Archbishop of Canterbury. Thus in the context of whether or not there was a re-marriage, here is a clear statement that there was, with a future Archbishop officiating and two great Statesmen as witnesses. And it was the Lord Chief Justice himself who had personally seen it and referred to it. As to the matter of why Chatham and Dunning should appear yet again as witnesses, they had been 'in the know' concerning the Hannah Lightfoot affair from the outset, had proved their discretion about the matter, and were men of the right stature for such an important and significant occasion.

Both George IV and his wife Queen Caroline seem to have held the view that the original marriage was not valid. George, as has been previously noted, often taunted his parents over his birth; and Caroline also seems to have shared the view that the second marriage was not only necessary but did take place, as the following indicates:

The anonymous "*An Historical Fragment relative to Her late Majesty Queen Caroline*", published in 1824 soon after the Queen's trial for her alleged adultery, records that Caroline used to say that she was neither wife nor Queen. For she believed, according to this story, that regardless of the Royal Marriage Act, her husband George IV had been properly married to Mrs FitzHerbert so that she (Caroline) was not his proper wife. Also that the late King George III had been married to Hannah Lightfoot prior to his marriage to Queen Charlotte; that his second ceremony of marriage to Charlotte, although it occurred after the death of Hannah

Lightfoot, was also after the birth of their two eldest sons George and Frederick, so that she, Caroline, really considered William (later, William IV) Duke of Clarence as the true King, not her husband George. Whether this story about Caroline is true or not, its date (1824) clearly shows the extent of the contemporary knowledge of George and Charlotte's re-marriage.

So there are two possibilities concerning the date of George and Charlotte's re-marriage. *First* is the general awareness of the event, evidenced by extract quoted above concerning Queen Caroline, which supposedly took place at Kew in the summer of 1765 and was presided over by Dr Wilmot. *Second* is the letter referred to by the Lord Chief Justice, in which the re-marriage is stated to have occurred in January 1765, though now presided over by Dr Moore. The event itself, in both versions, occurred soon after December 1764, when Hannah Lightfoot is said to have died. The January date is the more likely, not only because of the documentary evidence but also because one can believe that Queen Charlotte would have been anxious for it to have happened at the earliest possible opportunity.

This re-marriage of King George to Queen Charlotte, whilst not being proof of the original Lightfoot marriage, is a significant step towards it. After all, what other reason could there have been for it?

The documentary evidence. There were over 100 documents, of which seventy were presented in the Ryves trial. Some of these are in the text here, some others are in Appendix 1. From 1820, when Mrs Serres first published her story, the public responses to it were first of incredulity and then to accuse her of fraud and forgery; there is little doubt that this highly imaginative lady's many talents included a lot of the ingredients to become quite a successful forger and fraudster *had she so wished.* That she had some extremely unpleasant traits alongside her acknowledged charm is indisputable. But that she was ever a forger has never been established. Nowhere outside of this trial is any specific accusation made of forgery; ie what did she supposedly forge, when, for what purpose, how was the forgery discovered? The support for claims of forgery rests solely on the Ryves trial result. That Mrs Serres particularly, or anyone else for that matter could, for instance, monitor and forge the changing signatures over the years of so many people significant to her case is hardly a credible proposition. Of the free use of her imagination, of her inability even to tell a consistent story, her own writings are ample proof. But nowhere is there even any suggestion, let alone proof that she ever forged anything, not even when for instance, in dire financial straits, she might have been expected to produce from somewhere a piece of paper that proved someone owed her money or that some piece of property was hers. (The statement by her husband concerning a forged signature stands alone and isolated; and in any event has to be taken in context first with his own threatened imprisonment, and second with his equally unsupported claims in his Will about her alleged affairs and children). This is not to say that she *didn't* forge any of her documents, only that there is neither evidence nor proof of it. Even in the Fleet debtors prison she tried to work herself out of debt as far as she could by publishing various 'discoveries' and 'inventions'. And as far as the trial was concerned, the Crown had had many years to search out this kind of evidence. Nothing was found since none was presented.

In the trial many of the documents had been attacked because it was maintained that they had, largely, been written on 'scraps of paper', not on the watermarked sheets the Court seemingly expected for documents emanating from the Royal Family and others, and so must have been forgeries. Even superficial examination of the documents in the Public Records Office suggests that this 'scraps of paper' description, though derogatory, is reasonable. They are, generally, in poor condition. Many are torn, heavily creased from folding and multiple handling, have indecipherable letters or characters, and so on. And the papers themselves do not appear to be the kind of watermarked vellum quality sheets that the Judges seemed to expect. Many of them would probably have been written 'on the spot' to set down (and witness) a quick decision; they would then have been inspected, studied, manhandled and stored many times, over a period of some 100 years or so, in far from ideal circumstances. One of the British Library copies of *Flights of Fancy* has an original letter from Mrs Serres bound into the front. There is no question that this letter is not hers, yet it too is badly creased and torn and so would clearly qualify as one of the 'scraps of paper that no-one could believe in'. Not until they were handed over to the appropriate authorities after the trial were they ever carefully looked after. And on the matter of the quality of the sheets of paper, the Lord Chief Justice observed to Mrs Ryves that the Duke of Kent seemed to have been as poor to paper as the Earl of Warwick: "Yes" she replied, "He was very fond of scraps." And in her *Princess Olive,* Margaret Shepard observes in a footnote that *The family of George III were notorious for writing innumerable notes on cheap writing paper.*

Much of the time of the Court had been given to the matter of forgery, and in particular to the question of the signatures. These signatures had been supported, in sworn evidence by both expert and laymen, to be those of whom they purported to be. In his opening statement to the Court Dr Smith noted that seventy documents would be introduced and these would bear forty three of Dr Wilmot's signatures, thirty six of Pitt's (or Chatham's), twelve of Dunning's, thirty two of Warwick's, eighteen of Kent's, and twelve of George III's; Netherclift declared all of these to be genuine excepting only one of Dunning's (and this on a minor document) of which he was doubtful. However hard the Attorney General tried, and he tried very hard, he could not alter that, yet he was adamant in his closing speech that forgery had to be the answer. In his own summing up the Lord Chief Justice, still describing these signatures as 'spurious', stated that the documents themselves were not believable; that in certain examples *even if the evidence of the signatures and handwriting could be accepted,* still no-one could believe they were genuine (the 'scraps of paper' point). It was not possible to believe, he said, that the documents produced to the Court were those that might have been shown previously to members of the Royal Family and others who had stated their belief in them. Forgery had to be the answer. He did not however explain how possibly genuine handwritten texts and signatures might have come to appear on scraps of paper that no one could believe in.

Hannah Lightfoot's Will is one document that has been attacked as an obvious forgery. In his summing up the Lord Chief Justice, referring to the signature 'Hannah Regina', asked '(Is) it possible to imagine, even if such a person had ever existed and asserted her right to that title, that great Officers of State like Chatham and Dunning should have outraged all propriety by recognising that claim and putting their names to a document in which she assumed that title?' Yet, since their signatures had been authenticated by Netherclift and others, that question can be turned around to ask 'Is it possible to deny the title recognised by such great Officers of State?' And of course it is these same 'great Officers of State' who also witnessed so many of the other documents produced, and whose signatures were also quite independently supported. And here it is worth observing that the Lord Chief Justice himself, in that rhetorical question, referred to *Chatham's* name being on a 1762 document which actually had *Pitt's*, clearly Dr Smith's response about the use of 'Chatham' instead of 'Pitt' being 'a mode of speech' was well made.

The Will has also been separately, ie outside the Court proceedings, challenged (thanks ultimately to *The Morning*

Post) on the grounds that in it Hannah refers to her 'best friend Doctor Wilmot' in a document dated 1762, yet Wilmot supposedly did not attain his DD until 1766 according to the *Post*. Wilmot, it is argued, could not have been 'Doctor' for a 1762 document, but for a 1768 document, the date (also) inaccurately given to the Will by *The Post*, he would have been. This is taken as evidence of Mrs Serres' carelessness in forging the Will and then dating it 1762 when she should have dated it 1768 (as in the *Post*'s articles) to cover the Wilmot doctorate. However Wilmot actually obtained his doctorate in 1760 (the Archivists at Trinity College and at Oxford University both confirm this year for the award, the University Archivist giving the precise date as 5th July 1760). Hannah's description in 1762 of her 'best friend' as 'Doctor' is perfectly valid.

The Will has been further criticised because the signature has been written in a very shaky hand. Yet if Hannah Lightfoot was ill at the time, and this is often a reason for people to make a Will, there is a cause for a shaky signature; and since we have an indicative date for her death, at the early age of thirty four, as 1st December 1764, it may even have been this illness to which she eventually succumbed just 2½ years later. The Will *could* have been forged, of course, but not on the basis of these challenges, and no others have been offered.

But all this begs the question: who would be interested in forging this particular document? Mrs Serres had absolutely no interest in the Lightfoot affair. She was concerned only to establish her own Royal credentials and inheritance, and all the Lightfoot Will did for her was to say that Hannah was a friend of her mother Olive Wilmot, and of her grandfather Dr Wilmot.

Other documents are similarly queried. The 1767 marriage certificate of Cumberland to Olive Wilmot (Appendix 1: No 8) states that the witnesses were Brooke (ie Warwick), and J. Addez about whom there is anyway a certain lack of clarity. There is a PRO file containing a letter written by Lord Warwick on 21ˢᵗ June 1822 to King George IV in which, referring explicitly to this certificate he states: 'My Grandfather did not die till the year 1773 prior to which my Father was <u>always</u> Lord Greville, he never (was called or) signed his name Brooke during his Father's life & consequently as the signature to this marriage must be incorrect, I venture to lay the above statement before your Majesty.' (This letter indicates that Mrs Serres' early claims for recognition had received at least some attention at the highest level).

Nevertheless not all the documents can be straightforwardly accepted or rejected. Without necessarily attaching an accusation of forgery to them, many can still be queried and perhaps regarded with some degree of suspicion. For instance the separate testaments of Edward Duke of Kent apparently leaving property and assets to Mrs Serres, and appointing her to be the guardian of his daughter Victoria, are dubious to say the least. The Public Records Office files contain (a copy of?) the Duke of Kent's last Will and

Testament written, signed and witnessed in the final days of his life. Everything is left to his wife and daughter, and the Duchess of Kent is appointed as Victoria's sole guardian, all of which is no more than one would have expected. But the point here is that there is *no mention whatsoever of Mrs Serres*, in any of her styles of cousin, duchess or princess, even although only a few months earlier there is the document appointing her as his daughter's guardian, and others leaving her property. Of course the Duke was a very sick man (he died within a few days of making this Will) and may well have overlooked many things he would otherwise have wished to add. And it is perfectly commonplace to write a new Will that would invalidate an earlier one. This final Will doesn't make those earlier Testaments false, but its complete omission of any reference to Mrs Serres doesn't do anything for her case.

The document in which George leaves £15,000 to Cumberland's daughter Olive cannot be a forgery since it is so strongly attested to, even to the declaration that it was actually written by the Earl of Warwick. Similarly, others are not suspect, being firmly supported by the trial evidence of leading handwriting expert Mr Netherclift. (In a completely unrelated matter, he was, in 1885, referred to in a learned journal as 'the chief caligraphic expert in England'). The most convincing element is where Mrs Serres provided, in 1822, the support to these witness signatures to this legacy to his niece, Cumberland's daughter Olive (ie to herself). Those sworn statements made in 1822 as to the authenticity of this document were made by unimpeachable witnesses. Each was properly sworn in front of a Notary Public and a witness. Yet they were simply included in the general sweeping allegations of fraud and forgery. But this document of George's could not have been forged. It is worth closer analysis:

George R. St. James's
In case of our Royal demise, we give and bequeath to Olive, our brother of Cumberland's daughter, the sum of £15,000, commanding our heir and successor to pay the same, privately, to our said niece, for her use, as a recompense for the misfortune she may have known through her father.

June 2, 1774.

Witness: J. Dunning.
                                               Chatham.
                                               Warwick.

In the few words of this document, the King first quite bluntly declares Olive to be his brother's daughter. He then refers to 'the misfortune she may have known through her father'. To what misfortune is he referring? That she might, for instance, be his brother's illegitimate daughter? Given the sexual promiscuity of the Hanovers and the number of Royal bastards around, this could hardly have concerned him. In any event another of his brothers, William, had also had an illegitimate daughter (Louisa Maria), and there has never been any suggestion that his daughter too was provided for in this way. The 'misfortune' is clearly the result of the damage limitation exercise that George himself was forced into when brother Cumberland bigamously married Mrs Horton, the exercise which deprived the future Mrs Serres of her rightful status.

The signatures of George himself, Dunning and Warwick are fully certified. In context Chatham's may be equally regarded, particularly in view of the following affidavit, which was sworn twenty-eight years later in 1850:

"I William Stanhope Taylor, of Howard Lodge, Tunbridge Wells, in the county of Kent, Esquire, do solemnly and sincerely declare that being as executor of the last Earl of Chatham, in possession of the family papers, and in which papers contain a great number of documents in the handwriting of, and signed by the first Earl of Chatham, I feel myself able to speak with confidence as to the signature of the said first Earl of Chatham. That I have carefully inspected and examined the paper writings or certificates now produced and shown to me, of which the following are true copies."

There follow two certificates concerning the marriage of Cumberland to Olive Wilmot on 4th March 1767, the second adding the sentence 'Olive the daughter of Henry Duke of Cumberland, and Olive his lawful wife, born April 3rd 1772 at Warwick.' A declaration by 'George R.', to the same effect as this sentence, with an additional comment concerning her father's bigamy. Chatham's promise to pay £500 yearly to the baby Olive until a more suitable provision is made for her. And Dr Wilmot certifying that he married the Princess of Poland 'and had legitimate issue Olive my dear daughter...'

"And I, this declarant, say that I verily believe the signature 'Chatham' affixed to each of the foregoing paper writings or certificates to be the proper handwriting and signature of the said first Earl of Chatham. And I make this solemn declaration, conscientiously believing the same to be true...etc"

Sworn before Wm. Stone, A Master extraordinary in Chancery 31st May 1850.

William Stanhope Taylor was Joint Editor, with Captain John H Pringle, of the four volume *Correspondence of William Pitt, Earl of Chatham* which they published in 1840. He was thus able to claim, 'with confidence' as he indicated, his familiarity with Chatham's signature.

Note too that the 'Warwick' signature was given in 1774, a year *after* the Earl had inherited his title and, even according to his son, would then have been using this style and have stopped signing as 'Greville' (or even 'Brooke'). Is it possible to doubt that King George did therefore leave this legacy of £15,000?

It is no great step to go from there to the other documents on the matter of Olive Wilmot, which bear *these* signatures and to accept, therefore, that these too must be genuine. The witnesses to the legacy document, Dunning, Warwick, and Pitt are the same men (two of them 'great Officers of State') who witnessed many of the other critical documents presented, including those concerning the Cumberland/ Wilmot marriage. The witnesses to this are Dunning and Chatham (Pitt) again, and also Brooke and Addez. 'Brooke' of course is the Earl of Warwick before he inherited this title though it is known that in 1822 his son wrote to the King with reference to this particular certificate saying that his father never signed anything as 'Brooke.' However in 1850 William Taylor authenticated Chatham's signature on this very same document, which seems to support the others. Of four signatures on the marriage certificate, only one is disputed. The Cumberland/Wilmot marriage is authenticated simply because the witnesses to it are the same people who were familiar with the later circumstances of this marriage, and who witnessed George's legacy to Olive Cumberland, the child of the marriage. And of course, Netherclift authenticated their signatures anyway.

On the matter of the 'Chatham' signatures, and in particular that on the Cumberland/Wilmot marriage, some very specific criticisms have been made by Mr W J Thoms; he was a celebrated antiquarian, man of letters, and Deputy Librarian to The House of Lords. He was also a critical disbeliever of the whole Lightfoot affair who stated that 'the story of Hannah Lightfoot is a fiction, and nothing but a fiction, from beginning to end.' He even denied that she had ever lived, although he had later to withdraw that opinion.

He pointed out that 27th May 1759, the date of the second Lightfoot marriage ceremony, was a Sunday. Not only was this an unlikely choice of day for Prince George, Thoms suggests, but since Chatham's son was born the following day, perhaps it was unlikely for him too. This is hardly a strong point; one can just as easily suggest that Sunday might have been a good day for George for a clandestine arrangement that would not interfere with any Royal duties. And Mr Thoms doesn't have anything to say about the earlier 12th April signature.

On the Cumberland/Wilmot marriage of 4th March 1767, Mr Thoms notes that on the preceding day (3rd March) Chatham had to have his wife write to the King apologising that he was 'not well enough to attend his Majesty's most gracious presence.' (He was recovering from an attack of gout). On the 7th March the King wrote to Chatham: 'I cannot conclude without desiring to learn how you continue, and insisting on your not coming out till you can do it with safety.' No references there, as Mr Thoms notes, to their supposed meeting on the 4th, at Lord Archer's house for the wedding of George's brother, at which George was supposed to be present and Chatham a witness. This correspondence indicates that it was unlikely (though not impossible) that both he and the King were at the marriage of Cumberland to Miss Wilmot. Thoms' inference is clearly that therefore Chatham wasn't there, so could not have signed as a witness, and thus the document must have been forged. However it is equally possible that Chatham was there and the King was not. Although it is always said that George attended his brother's private wedding at Grosvenor Square, there is no evidence that he did. (And he certainly was not present at Cumberland's second marriage.) Both Netherclift and W S Taylor however have authenticated Chatham's signature, so it is clear that *he* was there.

Referring to George's creation of Olive Wilmot as Duchess of Lancaster on 21st May 1773 (Appendix 1: No 17) Mr Thoms observes that Chatham wrote on 24th May, from his home in Burton Pynsent, in Somerset, of 'our very welcome guest, Lord Stanhope, who left us on Friday last.' The 24th May was a Monday notes Mr Thoms, therefore 'Friday last' was the 21st and since on that day Chatham must have been in Burton

Pynsent he could not have countersigned the Royal Warrant at St James's. However there seems no apparent reason why Chatham should not have left his guest a day or two early in order to travel to London to transact affairs of State (which no doubt would have involved more than just witnessing one of the King's documents), leaving Lord Stanhope in the care of Lady Chatham. He similarly attacks, on the basis of Chatham's serious indisposition at the time, his signature to Hannah's will. This criticism however is worthless since it is based on the supposed 1768 date of the will.

And on the reverse of these Cumberland/Wilmot certificates, as indicated earlier, are Dr Wilmot's affirmations of the marriage of George to Hannah Lightfoot confirming the certificates signed in 1759, with Dunning again signing as a witness. Dunning and Pitt (Chatham) are witnesses to Hannah's will. And Pitt also witnessed both of Dr Wilmot's certificates of the marriage of George to Hannah Lightfoot.

The Earl of Warwick (Brooke) was a distinguished Peer, the Earl of Chatham (Pitt) a great Minister of State and Prime Minister, and Dunning a very well known lawyer and later Solicitor-General. All were men of high distinction. No doubt sample signatures of these people could have been found and copied. The probability, however, of forging so many, so often, allowing for changes over the years, and doing this well enough to fool not only Mr Nethercott but also lesser men who had seen these signatures many, many times over periods of many years, must be remote unless the forger, and the only candidate here is Mrs Serres, had a truly exceptional talent in this direction. And as has been noted, other than her husband's allegation, no doubt made in a justifiable fury at the way she transferred to him the financial responsibility for her lifestyle, there has never been any separate evidence produced to show that she ever forged anything; indeed if there were, one could be sure that the Attorney General (and the Judges) would have exploited it to the full. There had been plenty of pre-trial 'discovery time' to have found such evidence, had it existed. Not even when she was desperately short of money is she accused of having forged any documents that might have helped her out. The letter that is bound into the British Library's copy of Mrs Serres' *Flights of Fancy* is interesting in this context. It is very carelessly written, with crossings out and insertions, and in handwriting of poor legibility. Her good friend and correspondent, the Earl of Warwick, had complained to her about her handwriting '...Be so good as to write legibly...'. The 'Warwick' files at the Warwick Records Office contain many examples of her untidy scrawl. Illegible handwriting does not seem to be a characteristic to be expected of someone who, in another facet of her life, was a skilled forger. And then there is her *Manifesto...to...the Kingdom of Poland*, (Appendix 4) which at least we know also really was hers. Is it possible that this rambling, incoherent piece of nonsense came from the same mind that, supposedly, created such an intricate fraud?

The correspondence concerning Robert Owen's advances to Mrs Serres (Appendix 1: Nos. 24,25,26) on behalf of the Duke of Kent is interesting. If these letters, and the correspondence implicit within them, were forged, they were good enough not only to convince the Queen and her advisers, who instantly paid up on the evidence provided, but also Robert Owen's son who could be expected to recognise his father's handwriting. But if they are genuine, they provide further evidence in favour of Mrs Serres' claims, ie that the Duke of Kent was supporting her financially (through Mr Owen) to the tune of £400 pa. And the fact that the Queen paid up almost without a murmur and kept the documents is sufficient proof of the circumstances to which they relate.

In any event there are more than enough fully validated documents that were presented and/or examined at the trial to show that the Cumberland/Wilmot marriage, with all its consequences, did happen. And therefore so did the George/Hannah marriage.

Among the documents *not* presented at the Ryves trial was the letter which the Lord Chief Justice had seen that 'certified' the re-marriage and which seems to me to be a very significant item; since it was not presented in evidence (again: why not?) does this mean that it was excluded from the allegation of collective forgery? Also excluded were letters from the Duke of Kent to Mrs Serres saying that he had seen her Hannah Lightfoot papers. These were not presented because they had been suppressed, in 1865, by order of the Prime Minister, Earl Russell.

The conduct of the trial. It has already been noted that this trial was one that the Crown could not afford to lose. This was not because of the possible financial claims of £1m (or more), which would hardly have been a problem either for the Queen personally or the Treasury. It was because of the consequences of the Hannah Lightfoot marriage being shown to have happened. The Crown pulled out all the stops to ensure that Mrs Ryves' lightweight legal team was not going to win. For instance, even though it would have been known to the Attorney General that the Duke of Kent *had* arranged financial support for Mrs Serres, he dismissed Mrs Ryves' Counsel's attempt to make this point as 'pure fiction'. Why did he further degrade the Court process with this lie? Of itself this financial prop provided by Kent did little for Mrs Ryves' case; it could have been interpreted to suggest that the Duke might have been too gullible, yet the Attorney General was prepared to lie in order not to concede even that small point. And why, when the case was already won, did he say that he was prepared to prove that Dr Wilmot could not have carried out the Cumberland/Olive Wilmot ceremony because he was in Oxford on that day and the following day? The answer surely must be that he wanted only to convince further any possible doubters who had been following the case. Yet this claim, had it actually been put forward in the trial could have been easily disproved, as Dr Smith said in immediate response; but it was too late. To the Crown it didn't really matter whether or not the Duke of Cumberland had married Olive Wilmot, or whether their daughter Mrs Serres was entitled to call herself a princess, a duchess or anything else. The problem was that the proof of her claim carried the evidence that George III had married Hannah Lightfoot, so it had to be shown to be worthless. Even the Special Jury is suspect: why would a Jury wish to stop a trial before hearing the final arguments for *both* sides? And worse, why would the Presiding Judge seem to support this move? But whilst the trial reached its predetermined conclusion, it didn't convince anyone that it had arrived at the truth. Perhaps for that reason the Court was not prepared to allow anybody else to have a look at the evidence, ordering it all to be locked away. Amid all the claims of fraud to be found in this trial, the biggest fraud was the trial itself. And this itself makes a very strong argument that George, Prince of Wales, did indeed marry Hannaḥ Lightfoot.

Together the re-marriage of King George to Queen Charlotte, the documentary support to the various events related, and the conduct of the Ryves trial provide *at the very least* the *'reasonable proof'* that most trial enquiries look for: that on 12ᵗʰ April 1759 George Prince of Wales married Hannah Lightfoot and that, therefore, on 25ᵗʰ October 1760, on the death of King George II, she became Queen Hannah and so was truly, **Hannah *Regina*.**

Hannah's (supposed) Children

Hannah had three children, two sons and a daughter; she said so herself, and Dr Wilmot confirmed this. There are no firm details of who was the eldest, nor whether he/she was born before or after she and George married. She is always described as having been George's mistress before becoming his wife, yet this description is open to a challenge which would enhance a claim to the throne on behalf of whichever of her two sons had been the first born. There are two quite independent sources, Mr William Beckford and Dr Wilmot, who seem to suggest that she may never have been George's mistress; that perhaps the relationship was not consummated until after they married.

<u>Mr William Beckford</u> was one of the wealthiest and most talented men of his time (1760-1844), though subjected to virtually total exclusion from Society for his open homosexuality; his wealth was inherited from his father, a remarkably successful self-made man who had been twice Lord Mayor of London. William Beckford is best known now for his novel *Vathek* and for having transformed Fonthill Abbey into a huge and lavishly expensive home with a 300ft tower providing magnificent views across the Wiltshire countryside, though very little of it now remains. His exclusion from Society was so complete that when, in 1800, he gave a grand opening party at Fonthill, almost the only notable people present were Lord Nelson and Lady Hamilton, who had themselves so outraged society. In 1840, then aged eighty but still in very sound mind, he gave interviews to a

journalist in which, in the context of being asked about Lady Anne Hamilton's book *Secret History of the Court of England,* he said

"George III, when Prince of Wales, fell in love with a beautiful Quakeress of the name of Hannah Lightfoot. . . . *As the Prince could not obtain her affections in exactly the way he most desired,* [my italics] he persuaded Dr Wilmot to marry them, which he did at Kew Chapel, in 1759, William Pitt, afterwards Lord Chatham, being one of the parties witnessing and, for aught I know that document is still in existence."

It is still in existence, as has been seen. And note that not only was this was said in 1840, well before the publicity of the Ryves trial, but Beckford was not quoting a rumour; he clearly *knew* of the marriage, who performed it, and who was one of the witnesses. However the point here is Beckford's phrase, which I have italicised. Can this mean anything other than that Hannah refused a sexual relationship until they were married? As a healthy young woman she would no doubt have wanted a full relationship with George but, as a very religious woman, perhaps she would have consented to it only within marriage. She would have been raised with a deep belief in the absolute truth of the Bible and have been well aware of St. Paul's maxim that sexual intercourse is intended solely for procreation *within* marriage.

Dr Wilmot (Appendix 1: No 23), wrote in January 1789:

I solemnly certify to the Parliament of England that I married George Prince of Wales to Princess Hannah his First Royal Consort April 17, 1759, and that three children were *lawfully* [my italics] begotten on the said Princess Hannah's Body (two sons and a daughter).

This is quite explicit. 'Lawfully' in this context, particularly to a clergyman such as Dr Wilmot, can only mean 'within marriage'. Of course this doesn't exclude a mistress relationship, but in purely practical terms that seems unlikely if all the children were 'lawfully' born, ie after they married. Wilmot also confirms, (in certificates 12,13, 'Lavinia Ryves' chapter), that the *issue of such marriage* were 'two princes and a princess' (12), or 'two sons and a daughter' (13).

Also, the likely dates of birth of the two men who might most possibly have been her sons are both around 1759/60; given the unreliability of birth control methods at the time, it seems quite likely that Hannah did refuse a sexual relationship, at least until she might have been virtually assured by George's promise of marriage.

Various accounts are given of the names, dates of birth, and of what may have happened to these children; there is no certainty about any of these accounts. The most widely believed story about any of them concerns George, supposedly given the surname Rex, and thought to have had a younger brother John, and a sister Sarah.

George Rex: He received some legal training, and was a Proctor at Doctors Commons from 1789 until 1797, but little else is known about his early life and upbringing. King George III is supposed to have taken an interest in him, though this interest seems to have hit a problem when young George was in his mid-thirties, since he was then effectively banished to South Africa. He said he was thirty six, having been born in 1760. He arrived in Cape Town in October 1797, with the appointment of Marshal of the Admiralty Court there, an appointment for which his experience as a Proctor in Doctors Commons would have been particularly useful. This was a lucrative position, which had the responsibility, amongst others, of dealing with captured naval Prize ships. The Warrant and Letters Patent of his appointment, signed by King George, state that this was *'in consideration of the Good and Public service already performed and which shall hereafter be performed for us by George Rex, Gentleman and for certain other good and lawful causes moving us in his behalf.'* He arrived also carrying some personal property, which supposedly closely identified him with the King. On his arrival he was also appointed Notary Public to the Governor. One of the stories about him is that before he left England he was required to promise that he would never return, and that he would never marry. True or not, he never returned and did not marry, though he had long-term relationships with two women. In 1801, after four years in his post he resigned it in order to develop an estate of his own choosing. This had been granted, together with an allowance, by the Crown, and he had selected a 4,000 acre estate in Knysna, some 150 miles east of Cape Town. He developed this huge estate, built a substantial house, was treated 'royally' wherever he went, that is as the 'legitimate' heir of King George, and lived out his life in considerable luxury. He had four children by the first, and nine by the second of the two women with whom, in turn, he lived, but refused to marry either of them. He never discussed his private life or origins with anyone, leaving the source of his wealth undefined though strongly suspected locally, and is even said to have burned his own papers rather than risk them being seen by others. He died in April 1839. But by 1801 it had been widely accepted in Cape Town, and seemingly still is, that he was the legitimate son of George III by Hannah Lightfoot. (This belief in 1801 is just another indication of how widespread were the rumours, and beliefs, in the marriage of George and Hannah.) Another Government employee of the time, a Mr Twistle, complained to his sister Mrs Dacres, in England about the favouritism shown to this Mr Rex being because he was *'the legitimate heir of our King, for his mother, the Quaker, and King George were joined in marriage before ever Queen Charlotte was thought of.'* Mr Twistle told his sister that Charlotte had insisted that the King go through a second marriage with her when she heard that the Quaker was dead (though one wonders how he came to hear of this), and that George Rex knew all about this and had used this knowledge to ensure that he himself was well provided for, and that George Rex didn't care for his lifestyle and wanted something better, like an estate with an income so he didn't have to work at his Government post. (Margaret Shepard, *Princess Olive.*) A letter in *Notes and Queries* of February 1861 has the following from a Mr William Harrison:

I was at the Cape of Good Hope in 1830 and spent some time at Mr George Rex's hospitable residence at the Knysna. I understood from him that he had been about thirty four years in the colony and I should suppose he was about sixty eight years of age, of a strong, robust appearance, *and the exact resemblance in features to George III.*

However there was a London distiller, a gentleman from Whitechapel named John Rex, whose existence, and family tree have been firmly established. He had three surviving children, George, John and Sarah. His eldest son, George, was born in September 1765, became a Proctor at Doctors Commons, and went to Capetown in 1797. This John Rex said in his Will that, having already given substantial sums to George, he left the rest of his property to John and Sarah; this suggests an alternative source for the wealth of George Rex of Knysna. There are other stories concerning the arrival of a George Rex in Pennsylvania USA, where there are a number of families claiming descent from George III through this supposed son. This claim has been shown to be faulty, from an examination of the Pennsylvania Archives, which suggests that the George Rex concerned was probably of Swedish origins.   .

George Rex of Knysna was a solid, indisputable character who left substantial property, a large family, and a significant mystery behind him as to whether he was Hannah's son by George III, or was the son of John Rex the Whitehall distiller. However, a study in the early 1970's by Professor Ian Christie of University College, London, showed quite clearly that George Rex of Knysna was the son of John Rex. Even so, there is still something of a mystery. How did this son of an otherwise unknown London merchant come to bear such a seemingly very close resemblance to George III? What 'Good and Public service' had the distiller's son performed for the King? It must have been very significant indeed for him to have been allowed to choose for himself such a huge estate.

If he *had* been George's son by Hannah, and born in 1760 as he is supposed to have claimed, he would probably have been their second son, but legitimate, ie born after they married, and therefore George III's legitimate heir. But he was not. John Rex the distiller's children, who appear in some respects at least to have been 'adopted' by some searchers for Hannah's children, do not have the Royal blood.

John Rex, another supposed son of Hannah's, and brother of George, leaves no stories other than that he is supposed to have married, and died young, possibly at sea, leaving one, possibly two children. Attempts to identify this John with John Mackelcan (see below) can be entirely discounted.

Sarah Rex, supposed daughter of Hannah and sister of George and John, is said to have lived most of her life in Bath without financial concerns, and remained single, though apparently staying in touch with her brothers. This lady died, in Bath, in 1842. It is also the case that Sarah the distiller's daughter lived in Bath, and died there in 1842, leaving £1000 to be divided between her nieces and nephews in South Africa. After her elder brothers, Sarah Rex would have been a possible heir to the throne. But Hannah Lightfoot's children, whoever they were, were not called George, John, and Sarah Rex.

However a seemingly far more promising candidate even than George Rex as a possible son of Hannah's is:

John Mackelcan who is thought to have been the adopted
son of John and Sarah Mackelcan, of Surrey; they baptised a
boy, John, on 12ᵗʰ April 1759 (ie the day that George and
Hannah married). In 1773, this boy, at the age of fourteen,
entered the Army taking a position in the Drawing Office of
the Royal Engineers. By 1795, at the age of just thirty-six, he
had become a full General in the Engineers. It was
commonplace then to use money, influence or both to obtain
promotion, but from his origins John Mackelcan seemingly
had neither. As an engineer there were not too many
opportunities to display exceptional brilliance in the field, this
latter being another route for fast promotion; his army
service however was mainly during a period of peace. So how
was this astonishing career achieved? Even Colonel Horton,
Anne Horton's brother, with all his advantages of birth, wealth
and active service, didn't get to be a general until he was
forty-five.

When John Mackelcan was just ten, Lord Romney, a
prominent Peer of the time, introduced him to Christ's
Hospital. Soon after joining the Army at fourteen, he was
nominated to Woolwich Military Academy by the Earl of
Chatham. He moved rapidly through the army, his various
promotions all being properly posted in the records of the
Royal Engineers. General Mackelcan was said always to have
been very popular with the Royal Family. In 1814 he received
an annual allowance of £700 from the Prince Regent,
supposedly for giving up a claim to a battalion, even though
there were no battalions in the Engineers. How did all this
come about? How, *why,* did Lords Romney and Chatham (of

all people) come to share an interest in this young man of obscure origins? Why did the Prince Regent provide this allowance of £700 a year? General Mäckelcan always told his children about a chest of papers, which would explain, after his death, his remarkable career. But when he died, these papers could not be found.

Many of these questions find answers if he was George's son by Hannah Lightfoot. He gives his date of birth (in army records) as March 1759, which is some four to five weeks *before* Hannah married George on 17th April, or ten to fifteen weeks before their second ceremony on 27th May. These dates make it clear that, even if he were George's son by Hannah, neither he nor any of his descendants (he married and had children) could ever have been legitimate claimants to his father's throne. But was he a son of this marriage?

Three American brothers named Mackelcan have gone to great lengths to establish their direct descent from the General and have produced a family tree which demonstrates this. A TV production company has used this evidence to test the theory that the General might have been King George's son by Hannah Lightfoot. They were able to obtain a DNA sample from one of George's UK descendants about whose family line there could be absolutely no doubt, and this was compared with DNA samples provided by these American Mackelcans. The test results showed that there was virtually no possibility that the American Mackelcans could have descended from George; so, despite his remarkable career, General John Mackelcan was not a son of George III. This

DNA procedure was also used with some of George Rex's current living descendants in South Africa, and also with another claimant family called Rex in Australia. Again the tests showed virtually no possibility of descent from King George, though in these cases that was no surprise.

Sir Samuel Park: He was a London merchant, born in 1760, who claimed to be Hannah's son by King George. He was, according to the story, created *Sir* Samuel by Act of Parliament and supposedly received £50,000 for 'suppressing the past'. He often stated he was the rightful King of England, (even though he was supposed to have received this very substantial sum not to say such things). He married an heiress named Sophie Fowler, and somewhere along the line changed his surname from 'Lightfoot' to 'Park'. Although there were Samuel(s) in the Lightfoot family tree, there is virtually nothing in the family history that substantiates these details of this person. There is no Act of Parliament that gave him a knighthood (why should it be necessary anyway?). He is not convincing as a son of Hannah, though there is some evidence to suggest that he might have been her cousin.

Sir Archibald Christie: From Chatham, in Kent, Sir Archibald was often spoken of, without any good reason, to have been one of Hannah's sons.

Captain John Ritso: Another favoured military officer who was thought to owe his appointments and preferments to a Hannah Lightfoot connection. In 1787 he arrived in India to serve, on the specific recommendation of Queen Charlotte, under General Cornwallis who wrote of him '...he is now writing in the Secretary's Office for 200 or 250 rupees a month, and I do not see the possibility of giving him anything better without deserving to be impeached.' If he was Hannah's son it seems unlikely that Queen Charlotte would have recommended him for anything, but since he was born in 1740 he couldn't have been a son of Hannah's since she was just ten years old at the time; he was probably related to...

Mrs Dalton: Née Catherine Augusta Ritso. The name Ritso is supposedly an Anglicisation of the continental Ritzeau; her parents were Frederick and Sophia Ritzeau who were private secretaries to Frederick, Prince of Wales and his wife Augusta, George's parents. Little is known of her other than that she was born in 1781, died in 1813, and in between married and had two children. Her husband was a Dr James Dalton, from Carmarthen, who went to work for the East India Company. He is referred to by Lord Wellesley, in a letter to Lord Bentinck, as being a brother-in-law of Captain Ritso, which suggests that the Captain was Catherine's brother. However in 1781, when Mrs Dalton was born, Hannah would have been fifty-one had she still been alive, and this alone makes her an unlikely candidate for royal status. But she has a popular following. The Dalton children, two girls, were called Charlotte Augusta and Caroline (George's mother was Princess Augusta, his second wife was Queen Charlotte). Their tombs were recently discovered in St. Peter's Church,

Carmarthen, found within a previously unknown vault with the inscription:

In this vault are deposited the remains of Charlotte Augusta Catherine Dalton, eldest daughter of James Dalton Esquire, formerly of this town and of Bangalore in the East Indies. She died on the 2ⁿᵈ day of August 1832, aged 27 years. Also, the remains of Margaret Augusta Dalton, second daughter of Daniel Prytherch, Esqr. of this town and of Abergole in this county by Caroline his wife, youngest daughter of the above James Dalton. She died on the 24ᵗʰ day of January 1839 in the Ninth Year of her age.

When the vault was opened there were found to be not two, but four coffins. Just another of the little mysteries surrounding the obscure Quaker girl who ran off with, and then, secretly married a Prince. It is interesting that this Prince, many years after he had become King, ordered a new organ for installation at Windsor, but later changed his mind and had it installed in this very same church of St. Peter's, Carmarthen. This 'coincidence' is currently being re-appraised in the light of the recent discovery.

Colonel Charles FitzRoy: He was a young man around George III's Court of whom it was said that he had been brought up as the son of Lord Southampton but was actually George's son by Hannah Lightfoot. It was also said of him that he had a liaison with, perhaps even married George's youngest child, Princess Amelia (1783-1810), who would have been his half-sister if he was George's son by Hannah. There is even mention of a child from the liaison. The promoters of this story also suggested that when the King came to hear of this, knowing of Fitzroy's origins, the news 'contributed greatly' to his madness. There is also a tale that a collection of Amelia's love letters was published in 1904, which would possibly have given clearer evidence concerning this relationship, but the entire edition was bought up, at a cost of £4-5,000, by King Edward VII, and suppressed. 'Fitz' of course is a prefix given to acknowledged, but not legitimate children of Royalty, and 'roy' would further suggest a royal connection. There is no evidence of his origins, nor of the supposed marriage (the liaison appears to have some substance), nor of the story concerning King Edward VII. His dates (1762-1831), allow the possibility that he *might* have been a son of Hannah's.

There is no shortage of names of people who have been suggested as Hannah's children by King George; their common quality is their lack of any convincing evidence. George Rex had credibility, but this was destroyed by Professor Christie's study; of those listed, the most interesting was General Mackelcan, but the DNA test has now eliminated him as one of George's sons.
As a result, there are now no real clues as to who Hannah's children may have been, nor what became of them.

11

Kew, and the Iron Chest

Kew Palace

Kew, and Kew Palace, now within the grounds of the world famous Royal Botanical Gardens founded by Princess Augusta, George's mother, and developed under his patronage was his favoured place. At Kew, only a short drive from London, he could escape from the atmosphere of the Court and from his grandfather, George II. He was out riding there when news of his grandfather's death reached him, bringing with it the knowledge that he was now the King. Over the subsequent years, many Royal events would take place there, either at Kew Palace or Kew Chapel, including his marriage to Hannah Lightfoot in 1759 (at the Chapel) and, it is said, his remarriage to Queen Charlotte at the Palace. The parish records since 1714, containing all the births, christenings, marriages, deaths, etc were all customarily stored in a large iron chest kept in a prominent position by the vestry of the Chapel.

The Times 26th February 1845: On Saturday February 23rd a little before nine in the morning the pew-opener found the vestry unlocked, went in and missed the iron chest from its accustomed stand on two wooden blocks. The thieves must have scaled the wall and picked the lock of the door. The iron chest contained all the parish records from 1717* to the present time. Plates, surplices, academic robes were untouched and no attempt had been made to enter the church.
* [A typographical error. Should be 1714].

In 1973 a Mr Arthur Lloyd-Taylor, who had been researching the history of his family, long residents of Kew, revealed in a privately printed book that according to family legend one of his ancestors, a Henry Taylor, had hired two men to break into the church at night, steal the iron chest, and take it back to his house on Kew Green. There, it was forced open and all the papers removed and handed over to whoever had commissioned this deed from him. The empty iron chest was then thrown over Kew Bridge into the River Thames. Taylor family history has It that this event, which was not spoken of openly within the family for many years, had to do with some member(s) of the Royal Family who wanted to conceal the record of an event or events that had taken place in the church or the parish.

Suppression, even theft, of papers is common in this whole Hannah Lightfoot affair. From impounding the Ryves trial papers, Lord Russell's suppression of Kent's letters, Queen Victoria's retention of the Robert Owen loan evidence, the disappearance of Joshua Reynolds' 'Sitters' book containing whatever details he may have recorded about his Patron for his *Mrs Axford* painting, the theft from Kew Chapel of the iron chest full of parish documents, the absence of papers belonging to one of the most convincing of Hannah's supposed children–John Mackelcan–after his death, and Dr Wilmot burning his papers before he died; even to the suggestion that Edward VII suppressed a book about George III's youngest daughter. Was all of this coincidental, or was there some kind of a pattern behind all of this? A pattern within which was woven a thread, in today's terms perhaps a virus, designed to obscure and conceal any evidence that might point a finger at the fact of George's marriage to Hannah Lightfoot.

The Royal Succession after Queen Hannah

The monarchical consequences of 'Queen' Hannah are reasonably clear. Much is determined by the precise date in 1765 of Queen Charlotte's remarriage to George III, and the validity of that ceremony depends on Hannah Lightfoot having died before then. There is a Lightfoot family legend that she lived to be 100; and there is a portrait, *supposedly* of her, showing a woman of about fifty. However, assuming the December 1764 date of Hannah's death, which fits well with the January (or even Summer) 1765 remarriage, this would clearly mean that George IV (born 12th August 1762) was *not* a legitimate King, as indeed both he himself and his wife Queen Caroline seem always to have believed. George and Charlotte's next son, Frederick Duke of York, was born on 16th August 1763, and was therefore also illegitimate but this is irrelevant since he died in 1827 before he could have succeeded his elder brother. Neither of these two sons of George had children who survived them. Next in line was William, Duke of Clarence, (born 21st August 1765), who succeeded George IV in the title of William IV. He was almost certainly legitimate because the Queen, clearly being heavily pregnant by midsummer, could be expected to have pushed for a remarriage date that would ensure the unborn child's legitimacy and of course a January remarriage would have ensured this. Edward, Duke of Kent (born 2nd November 1767) too would have been legitimate and it would then follow that Queen Victoria and all succeeding monarchs would have been legitimate. But if there were no remarriage, or if it took place after the Duke of Kent's birth, or if Hannah was still living at the time of Kent's birth (she would have been only 37), then all monarchs down to and including Queen Elizabeth II had no legitimate right to the throne. And if the Lightfoot family legend that Hannah lived to be 100 was true, then none of George and Charlotte's children were legitimate and the answer to the question of who might be today's rightful monarch would involve trawling through the descendants of first, George's father Frederick (who include the Duke of Cumberland), and perhaps even the other children of George II. The very clear probability, however, is that the present Monarch, Queen Elizabeth II, *is* legitimately entitled to rule.

Appendix 1 - Documentary Evidence
(a selection)

A. *Concerning Hannah Lightfoot:*

1. *April 17ᵗʰ 1759*

The marriage of these parties was this day duly solemnised at Kew Chapel according to the rites and ceremonies of the Church of England by myself. J. Wilmot

	George P.
	Hannah
Witness to this marriage -	W. Pitt.
	Anne Tayler.

2. *Hampstead July 7ᵗʰ 1762*

Provided I depart this life I commend my two Sons and my Daughter to the kind protection of Their Royal Father my Husband, His Majesty King George the Third, Bequeathing whatsoever property I may die possessed of to such dear offspring of our ill-fated marriage, In case of the death of my children I give and bequeath to Olive Wilmot the daughter of my best friend Doctor Wilmot whatever property I am entitled to or possessed of at the time of my death.

	Hannah Regina.
Witness:	J Dunning.
	William Pitt.

3. *London, April 2ⁿᵈ, 1760*
    This is to solemnly certify that I married George Prince of Wales to Princess Hannah his first consort, on April 17ᵗʰ, 1759, and that two princes and a princess were the issue of such marriage.

    J. Wilmot

4. The following are written consecutively on the same sheet of paper:

    I solemnly certify that I married George Prince of Wales to Hannah his first Royal Consort in the year 1759, and that such Royal personage departed this life December the first 17-4, leaving issue two sons and one daughter lawfully born in wedlock.

    J. Wilmot.

    I solemnly certify that Henry Frederick Duke of Cumberland was married to Olive Wilmot, March the 4ᵗʰ, 1767, in London, at Lord Archer's house, Grosvr. Square.

    J. Wilmot.

    Olive, the daughter of Henry Frederick Duke of Cumberland and Olive his wife, was born April the 3rd 1772, and is living.

    J. Wilmot.

    Lord Chatham confirms the above birth.

    Chatham.

The above certificates are written in this book for the securest mode of preserving the record of the same at Warwick Castle.   J W Warwick.

B.   *Concerning Olive Wilmot Serres* (Olive-2*)*

5.   I solemnly certify that I married the Princess of Poland and had legitimate issue Olive (Olive-1) my dear daughter married March 4ᵗʰ 1767 to Henry F. Duke of Cumberland brother of His Majesty George the Third who have issue my supposed *niece* born at Warwick April3rd 1772.   J. Wilmot.
G.R.   Robert Wilmot.
                                            Chatham.

6.   Olive my daughter by the Princess of Poland my wife born June 17ᵗʰ 1750.

                                            J. Wilmot.

7.   The marriage of the underwritten parties was duly solemnised according to the rites and ceremonies of the Church of England at Thomas Lord Archer's house London March the 4ᵗʰ 1767 by myself.

                                            J. Wilmot.
                                            Henry Frederick
                                            Olive Wilmot

Present at the marriage of these parties

                                            Brooke.
                                            J. Addez.

Attested before: J. Dunning.
                                            Chatham.

8. I solemnly certify that I married Henry Frederick Duke of Cumberland to Olive Wilmot March the 4ᵗʰ 1767 and that such marriage was lawfully solemnized at Thomas Lord Archer's house (at nine in the evening) in Grosvenor Square London. J. Wilmot.
    Witness to this marriage: Brooke.
    J. Addiz.
    Attested before: Chatham.
    J. Dunning.

9. Lords Chatham and Archer solemnly protest that the marriage of Henry Frederick Duke of Cumberland and Olive my daughter—the said Duke's present Duchess was solemnised legally at the latter nobleman's residence Grosvenor Square London by myself.
    J. Wilmot.
    Chatham.
    Archer.

    3rd. Novr. 1767
    These certificates never to be acted upon during His Majesty George the Third's reign—J.W.

10. We solemnly certify in this Prayer Book that Olive the lawful daughter of Henry Frederick Duke of Cumberland and Olive his wife bears a large mole on the right side and another crimson mark upon the back near the neck and that such child was baptised as Olive Wilmot at St. Nicholas Church by the

command of the King (George the Third) to save her royal father from the penalty of bigamy & c.

J. Wilmot.
Warwick.
Robt. Wilmot.

11. We hereby certify that Olive the Duke of Cumberland's infant was re-baptised in order that she might pass as the child of my brother Robert Wilmot and that such child of the Duke of Cumberland was entered in the register of St. Nicholas as Olive Wilmot only.

Robt. Wilmot.
J. Wilmot.

We hereby acknowledge having received to our joint protection Olive the infant child of the Duke of Cumberland April 4ᵗʰ 1772.

Robt. Wilmot.
Anna Maria Wilmot.
Witnesses —
J. Wilmot.
Warwick.

12. George/R. *May 1st 17*– We declare the birth of Olive the infant of the Duke of Cumberland by Olive his Duchess to bo legitimate who is condemned to privacy by an act of bigamy &c. committed by her royal father.

Warwick.
J. Wilmot.
Chatham.
J. Dunning.

13. "G.R. *April four 1772*
Whereas it is our royal will that Olive our niece be re-baptised Olive Wilmot to operate during our royal pleasure.

14. *Memo:* (undated).
That my brother Robert's wife having given birth to a still-born son, the same week that Olive, the wife of the Duke of Cumberland, was delivered of a daughter, it was determined that such child should be baptised as the infant of Robert Wilmot for a time.

J. Wilmot

15. "To Lord Chatham" *May 1ˢᵗ 1773*
I declare the Duke of Cumberland's marriage with Olive Wilmot to be legal by command of the King.

J. Dunning.

16. "G.R. *May 3ᵈ 1774*
In the face of Almighty God we the undersigned solemnly certify that His Majesty gave his royal command that Olive the legitimate daughter of Henry Frederick Duke of Cumberland by Olive his first wife should be re-baptised as the supposed child of Robert Wilmot of Warwick to save her royal father who had committed an act of bigamy by marrying Anne Horton.

J. Wilmot.
J. Dunning.

17. G.R.

"We are pleased to create Olive of Cumberland Duchess of Lancaster, and to grant our Royal authority for Olive, our said niece, to bear and use the title and arms of Lancaster, should she be in existence at the time of our Royal demise.

Given at our Palace of St. James's *May 21, 1773*

Chatham
J. Dunning

18. St. James's.

"George R. *June 2ⁿᵈ 1774*

In the case of our royal demise we give and bequeath to Olive our brother of Cumberland's daughter the sum of Fifteen thousand pounds commanding our heir and successor to pay the same privately to our said niece for her use as a recompense for the misfortunes she may have known through her father.

[Witness]   J. Dunning.

Chatham.
Warwick.

19. I solemnly certify that I privately was married to the Princess of Poland the sister of the King of Poland but an unhappy family difference induced us to keep our union secret. One dear child blessed myself who married the Duke of Cumberland March 4ᵗʰ 1767 and died in the prime of life of a broken heart December 5ᵗʰ 1774 in France.

Jany. 1st 1780

20. This is to declare that the Earl of Warwick has delivered in my presence the papers that confirm the birth of Olive Princess of Cumberland.   Edward.

Warwick.

London *July 17th 1815*

21. London *March 5ᵗʰ 1816*

I hereby make most solemn and sacred declaration that I saw his Majesty sign the papers that I have delivered to Mrs. Olive Serres of her birth.

Warwick.

On the reverse of this paper:

Lord Warwick's declaration of witnessing the Late King's signature.

John Dickenson

(This undated endorsement must have been written after the King's death in January 1820).

22. Kew Palace, *May2nd 1773*

Whereas it is our Royal command that the birth of Olive, the Duke of Cumberland's daughter, is never made known to the nation during our reign; but from a sense of religious duty, we will that she be acknowledged by the Royal Family after our death, should she survive ourselves, in return for the confidential service rendered ourselves by Dr. Wilmot in the year 1759.   George R.

Witnessed: Chatham.

Warwick.

Endorsed, London June 1815: Delivered to Mrs. Olive Serres by Warwick.

Witness: Edward.

23. Barton, *January 1789*
     I solemnly certify to the Parliament of England that I
     married George Prince of Wales to Princess Hannah
     his First Royal Consort April 17, 1759 and that three
     children were lawfully begotten on the said Princess
     Hannah's Body (two sons and a daughter).

     J. Wilmot

C. *Concerning Robert Owen:*

     (Robert Owen was a noted and wealthy English
     manufacturer and social reformer known as 'the
     father of British Socialism'; the Duke of Kent was
     President of one of his Committees and became a
     friend.)

24. Letter to the Duchess of Kent, following a draft
     dated *5ᵗʰ July 1840.*
     'Mr. Owen presents his respects to the Duchess of
     Kent...The late Duke of Kent communicated
     confidentially to Mr. Owen that the late Mrs. Serres
     was the legitimate daughter of his late uncle of
     Cumberland, and as such Mr. Owen paid her, at the
     particular request and on account of his Royal
     Highness the late Duke of Kent, an annuity of four
     hundred pounds per annum, which money, in
     consequence of the most unexpected death of the
     ever to be lamented Royal Duke, has never been
     repaid to Mr. Owen, who, out of a high regard to His

Royal Highness and in full confidence in his royal word, declined, when offered, to take legal security for its repayment. The object of Mr. Owen is not to bring forward any claim on his own.....'

25.   Recollections of Robert Owen, Esq., *21ˢᵗ July 1843*. (Probably provided to Mrs. Ryves in support of her case.)
'Being on friendly ...terms with His Royal Highness (the Duke of Kent) I was introduced about 1817 by him to Mrs. Serres as his cousin, the legitimate daughter of the Duke of Cumberland. His Royal Highness was at this period under some pecuniary difficulties, and he requested me, as I had then much wealth at my disposal, to lend him money to assist to support his cousin, to which I consented, and paid Mrs. Serres, as Princess Olive of Cumberland, various sums at various times amounting as far as my memory serves, before the Duke's death, to upwards of £1200....His Royal Highness offered to give me his notes...but I declined troubling him....The Duke's letters to me I took to America in 1826 and '27, intending to write my life there, but a multiplicity of business prevented me from making a commencement, and I left the letters there in chests with my sons.'

26.   Letter from Mr. Robert Dale Owen. (Son of Mr. Robert Owen.)
Cox's Hotel 55 Jermyn St. London. *Decr. 6 1858*

'Dear Mrs. Ryves—You state that my dear father advanced to your mother the Princess Olive Twelve hundred pounds on behalf of the late Duke of Kent and that this debt is still due by the duke's representatives. Have you any written proof that my father at the duke's request paid your mother this money? If you have it would be very important to me at this juncture to have it in the shape of a certified copy of the paper or papers* in question. Will it be convenient for you that I should call on you and if so at what hour. I shall remain probably two or three months in London. Hoping that the proceedings in the new Probate Court may be satisfactory...'

*(These papers may be the ones that were retained by the Queen after she had settled her father's debt to the Owen family).

27.   Extract from Robert Owen's autobiography:
'Here I must ...give some account of a branch of the Family...known as Mrs. Serres, afterwards as the Princess Olive of Cumberland, and now Mrs. Lavinia Ryves the only child of the latter. From the documents existing and carefully preserved, there can be no doubt of the legal claim of this family to their being the direct descendants of the Duke of Cumberland, brother to His Majesty George III, and entitled to his rank and property.'

Appendix 2 – Document Illustrations

1. The marriage of George to Hannah Lightfoot (17th April 1759)

2. The marriage of George to Hannah Lightfoot (27th May 1759)

3. Hannah Lightfoot's will (7th July 1762)

4. The Cumberland/Wilmot marriage (4th March 1767)

5. The Cumberland/Wilmot marriage (at nine in the evening)

6. The re-baptism of Cumberland's daughter Olive as Olive Wilmot.

7. George and Hannah's 'two Sons and a Daughter'.

April 17th 1759

The marriage of These Parties was this Day duely Solemnized at Kew Chapel according to the Rites and Ceremonies of the ... of ... by myself

Wilmot

witness to this marriage

W. P.

Anne Taylor

George P.

Hannah.

The marriage of George to Hannah Lightfoot(17th April 1759)

14

May 27th 1759

This is to Certify that the Marriage of his Royal..
(George Prince of Wales) to Hannah Lightfoot was
Duly Solemnized this Day according to the Rites
and Ceremonies of the Church of England at their
Residence at Peckham by Myself

Wilmot

George Guelph

Hannah Lightfoot

Witness to the Marriage
of these Parties:

William Pitt

Anne Taylor —

The marriage of George to Hannah Lightfoot (27th May 1759)

Hannah Lightfoot's will (7ᵗʰ July 1762)

Superscribed July 7th 1762

Provided I depart this Life Incircumstanced My Two Sons and
My Daughter is to The Kind Protection of their Royal Father
My Husband His Majesty George The Third, Bequeathing whatever
Property Ismay Die possessed of to such Uses or Issue of our
Sacred Marriage — In case of the Death of such My Children
I give and Bequeath to Such Issue the Survivors of my Best
Persons Court Richmond whatever Property I am entitled to
Physical or Circumstances my Death —

Witness —
[signature]
William [illegible]

Hannah Regina
[signature] Hannah, Regina.

The Cumberland/Wilmot marriage (4th March 1767)

The Cumberland/Wilmot marriage (4ᵗʰ March 1767)

May 3 — 1774.

In the Face of Almighty God do we the undersigned Solemnly Certify that His Majesty gave His Royal Command that Olive the Legitimate Daughter of Henry Frederick Duke of Cumberland by Olive his Born Wife should be rebaptized as the Wayward Child of Robert Wilmot of Warwick so now her Royal Father who had committed an Act of Bigamy by marrying Ann Horton — Dunning. Wilmot.

The re-baptism of Cumberland's daughter Olive as Olive Wilmot.

This is to Certify to all it may concern
that I lawfully married George Parrier
of Wales to ......nah Lightfoot April
the 17th 1759 and that two John and a
Daughter are Therefore by such
marriage.

W. Clayworth

Chatham

Denny

George and Hannah's 'two Sons and a Daughter'

Appendix 3 – The Royal Marriages Act 1772

Saint Edward's Crown

As a result of the problems created by the secret marriages of his brothers the Dukes of Gloucester and Cumberland, the King proceeded to force on to the statute books the *Royal Marriages Act*, which requires members of the Royal Family to obtain the Sovereign's permission to marry. His object was to ensure that there could be no similar dangers if later another relative, one of his own children for instance, decided on a secret or rushed marriage. This of course didn't stop two of his sons. The eldest, the future George IV, didn't ask his father's permission—he knew it would have been flatly refused—before secretly marrying Mrs FitzHerbert in 1785. Because she was a Roman Catholic, he was also deliberately ignoring the 1701 *Act of Settlement*, which forbade him to do this on pain of being debarred from the succession. Not surprisingly, he had some difficulty in finding a Minister to perform this marriage ceremony, since even participation in such an illegal arrangement carried its own penalties.

However the Rev. John Burt, currently in the Fleet debtor's prison (shades of Dr Keith!), in return for the settlement of his debts, a Chaplaincy, and the promise of a bishopric on George's eventual accession, agreed to act. His debts (some £500) were paid, he was released from prison, carried out the ceremony, and received his Chaplaincy, but died before George became King and could honour the last part of the agreement. At least with this marriage, George was not flouting the *Clandestine Marriages Act* of 1753, since the Royal family had been specifically excluded from its provisions. Ten years later, in 1795, just to show he was a real Hanover, he married again, this time publicly, to his cousin Princess Caroline of Brunswick (who became Queen Caroline in January 1820) whilst Mrs FitzHerbert was still very much alive and married to him. However because his marriage to Mrs FitzHerbert had contravened the recent *Royal Marriages Act*, it was illegal according to the Laws of England, (even though in 1800 it was officially recognised by the Pope); there was therefore no problem with the Act of Settlement, nor any question in English law of the marriage to Princess Caroline not being valid, so she was properly his Queen even though he quickly came to detest her, tried to prevent her attendance at his coronation, and arranged that she be tried for adultery.

Another of George III's sons, Augustus Frederick Duke of Sussex, on 4ᵗʰ April 1793 married Lady Augusta Murray in Rome, later that year confirming the marriage with another ceremony at St George's, Hanover Square. However the King, becoming aware through this re-marriage of his son's action, refused to recognise it and declared it illegal under the Royal Marriages Act. Nevertheless the Rome marriage remained legal since it was later determined that the provisions of the Royal Marriages Act were restricted to marriages contracted within Great Britain. His wife died in 1830, and in 1831 he married again, again in defiance of The Royal Marriages Act, though by now both George III and George IV had died and another brother, William Duke of Clarence, had become King.

The Royal Marriages Act states that:

No descendant of the body of his late majesty King George the Second, male or female, (other than the issue of princesses who have married, or may hereafter marry, into foreign families) shall be capable of contracting matrimony without the consent of his Majesty, his heirs, or successors, signified under the great seal, and declared in council, (which consent, to preserve the memory thereof is hereby directed to be set out in the licence and register of marriage, and to be entered in the books of the privy council); and that every marriage, or matrimonial contract, of any such descendant, without such consent first had and obtained, shall be null and void, to all intents and purposes whatsoever.

Provided always, and be it enacted by the authority aforesaid, that in case any such descendant of the body of his late Majesty King George the Second, being above the age of twenty-five years, shall persist in his or her resolution to contract a marriage disapproved or dissented from, by the

King, his heirs, or successors; that then such descendant, upon giving notice to the King's privy council, which notice is hereby directed to be entered in the books thereof, may, at any time from the expiration of twelve calendar months after such notice given to the privy council as aforesaid, contract such marriage; and his or her marriage with the person before proposed, and rejected, may be duly solemnised, without the previous consent of his Majesty, his heirs, or successors; and such marriage shall be good, as if this Act had never been made, unless both houses of parliament shall, before the expiration of the said twelve months, expressly declare their disapprobation of such intended marriage.

And be it further enacted by the authority aforesaid, that every person who shall knowingly or wilfully presume to solemnise, or to assist, or to be present at the celebration of any marriage with any such descendant, or at his or her making any matrimonial contract, without such consent as aforesaid first had and obtained, except in the case above-mentioned, shall, being duly convicted thereof incur and suffer the pains and penalties ordained and provided by the statute of provision and præmunire made in the sixteenth year of the reign of Richard the Second.

Appendix 4 – Manifesto to Poland

MANIFESTO
OF
OLIVE, PRINCESS OF CUMBERLAND,
TO THE
HIGH DIGNITARIES, PRINCIPALITIES,
AND
ECCLESIASTICAL POWERS OF THE KINGDOM OF POLAND,
AND
ITS BRAVE PEOPLE.

WHEREAS it has pleased Divine Providence to discover Our high and illustrious descent from your last reigning Sovereign; being the immediate Heir and Representative of AUGUSTUS STANISLAUS, your King, as well as the only Daughter and Representative of HENRY FREDERICK, late Duke of Cumberland, by Olive, his Duchess, the legitimate Daughter of the Princess of Poland, by JAMES WILMOT D.D., her lawful Consort. We, as aforesaid, allied and descended, claim your affectionate consideration and regard,–confident that so great and brave a Nation will afford its loyal protection to the last Heir of your glorious race of Kings!—by restoring to Us all or any of the claims of a public or private nature, that Our birth and Royal descent merits at the Kingdom of Poland's hands, whose subjects have so frequently distinguished themselves, and whose courage and virtues bear the proudest pre-eminence in the annals of historic record! Yes! Brave People, you will form a phalanx round the person of your injured Princess, and afford Us that aid Our unprotected situation, and injuries and deprivations render indispensable.—Thus, We appeal to your justice and sense of moral duty to aid the wonderful workings of Divine Providence, who has rent asunder the adamantine barriers of political oppression, and given to Our Royal knowledge the truth and facts that authorise Our address to you, beloved People of Poland. The mercy of Heaven having lead Us to the knowledge of mankind, such as We really are. — Believe Us, brave and injured people, when We assure you (well read in the vicissitudes of nations) that the welfare and independence of Poland is Our first prayer! And that in the deepest recesses of Our heart the beloved name of AUGUSTUS STANISLAUS holds its influence reanimating that hope that for too great a season has been annihilated by the despotism of ambition, policy, &c. — Politically educated to discriminate upon the conduct of the Powers of Europe, and devoted to the operative procedures of religious right, We declare that Our heart bleeds for the situation of a Country that should be proudly towering over the dependence that at this moment strikes at its most ancient and sacred liberties. Alas! beloved Nation of Our ancestors, your OLIVE lives but to anticipate the emancipation of Poland from cruellest degradation. Invite Us, then beloved People, to the Kingdom of Our ancestors, and the generous humanity and wise policy of ALEXANDER, will with religious justice yet restore to Us the Domain of Our ancient house, that his Majesty has only presided over for a season, in order that he might administer superior concord to secondary States.

We inform you, that Our legitimacy as Princess of Cumberland, has been proved according to law in England,

and that We have the most indisputable documents to satisfy the Principalities and High States of Poland of Our being OLIVE, the heir of AUGUSTUS STANISLAUS, and immediately allied to that great King by ties of blood.

OLIVE.

London, September 5, 1821,
        25, Alfred Place.

Appendix 5 – Who was Who

Hannah Lightfoot: Quaker girl (born 17th October 1730) living in London who was wooed and won by a much younger George Prince of Wales, later King George III.

Rev. Dr James Wilmot, MA DD: A Fellow of Trinity College Oxford. Said to have married Princess Poniatowski of Poland and to have had a daughter (Olive) by her.

Olive Wilmot: Supposed daughter of James Wilmot and his Polish princess.   Married (4th March 1767) the Duke of Cumberland as his first, and legitimate wife.

Henry Frederick, Duke of Cumberland: George III's youngest brother. Married (4th March 1767) Olive Wilmot (see above), and then (2nd October 1771) Anne Horton as his second, and bigamous wife.

George: Prince of Wales, born 4th June 1738, future King George III. On 11th December 1753, aged 15½, ran off with and later married (12th April 1759) Hannah Lightfoot, then married (8th September 1761) Princess Charlotte Sophia of Mecklenburgh-Strelitz.

Elizabeth Chudleigh: A Maid of Honour to Princess Augusta, Prince George's mother. Acted as principal procuress of Hannah Lightfoot for George. Later became famous/notorious as the Duchess of Kingston.

Mrs Olive Serres: Born 1772, supposed daughter of Olive Wilmot and the Duke of Cumberland. Brought up as the daughter of her great-uncle Robert Wilmot and as niece of James Wilmot. Around 1817 she first published her claim to be the daughter of Duke of Cumberland, granddaughter of James Wilmot, and niece to King George III.

Mrs Lavinia Ryves: Born 1797, daughter of Mrs Serres, and supposed granddaughter of the Duke of Cumberland. Initiated the famous lawsuit of 1866 (The Ryves trial) which, finally brought all these suppositions and 'said-to-be's' into open public examination.

Isaac Axford: Married Hannah Lightfoot on 11th December 1753, just before she eloped with Prince George.

'Dr' Alexander Keith: A charlatan priest in the Church of England who made a lot of money by exploiting the lax marriage rules of his time.

Robert Wilmot: Younger brother of Dr James Wilmot.

Mrs Olive Payne: Sister of Dr James Wilmot.

William Pitt: Statesman and Prime Minister. Later, Earl of Chatham. His signature appears on many of the documents in the Ryves trial either as Pitt, or Chatham (Earl of).

J Dunning: Well-known lawyer, appointed Solicitor-General in 1768, resigned on a point of principle in 1770; created Baron Ashburton in 1782. His signature appears on many of the Ryves trial documents.
Earl of Warwick: His signature appears on many documents, also sometimes as (Lord) Brooke.

Robert Owen: Noted British social reformer. He lent money to the Duke of Kent, who supported the claims of Olive Serres.

Robert Dale Owen: Eldest son of above. Noted American social reformer. Recovered his late father's loan from Queen Victoria, (the Duke of Kent's daughter)

Index

Bibliography

Anonymous: *An Historical Fragment relative to Her late Majesty Queen Caroline. London, 1824.*

Anonymous: *Authentic Records of the Court of England for the last Seventy Years. London, 1832.*

Aspinall, A (Ed):   *Letters of King George IV, Cambridge University Press, 1938.*

Bain, R. Nisbet: *The Last King of Poland. Arno Press, New York, 1971 reprint.*

Grant, Colonel Maurice Harold: *Old English Landscape Painters. F Lewis, Publishers, Ltd. Leigh-on-Sea. Revised Edn. 1953.*

Hibbert, Christopher: *George IV. London, Penguin, 1976.*

Hamilton, Lady Anne: *Secret History of the Court of England. W H Stevenson, 1832*

Keith, Alexander: *Observations on the Act for Preventing Clandestine Marriages. 1753*

Lindsey, John: *The Lovely Quaker. Rich & Cowan, Ltd. London, 1939.*

Lloyd-Taylor, Arthur: *The Taylors of Kew. Privately printed.*
Lloyd-Taylor, Arthur: *Appendix to The Taylors of Kew. Privately printed.*

Metelerkamp, Sanni: *George Rex of Knysna. Bailey Bros. and Swinfen, London, 1963.*

Osborn, J Lee: *Lainston and Elizabeth Chudleigh. Winchester.*

Pearce, Charles E: *The Amazing Duchess.   Stanley Paul & Co. London, 1911*

Pendered, Mary: *The Fair Quaker. Hurst & Blackett Ltd. London, 1910.*

Pendered & Mallett: *Princess or Pretender?   Hurst & Blackett, London, 1939.*

Price, C H: *George Rex: King or Esquire? Robert Hale and Co. London, 1974.*

Ryves, Lavinia: *An Appeal to Royalty: Being a Letter to her Majesty the Queen.   William Freeman, London, 2ⁿᵈ Edition, 1866.*

Serres, Olive: *Flights of Fancy. J Ridgway, London, 1805.*

Serres, Olive: *The Life of The Author of Junius' Letters, the Rev. James Wilmot DD. 1813.*

Serres, Olive: *Junius, Sir Philip Francis denied; a Letter to the British Nation. 1817.*

Serres, Olive: *Letters of the Earl of Warwick to Mrs Serres. London, 1819.*

Shepard, Margaret: *Princess Olive.   P Drinkwater, Shipston-on-Stour. 1984.*

Storrar, Patricia: *George Rex: death of a legend. Macmillan (SA), Johannesburg, 1974.*

Taylor and Pringle: *Correspondence of William Pitt, Earl of Chatham. 1840.*

Thoms, W J: *Hannah Lightfoot*

Walpole, Horace: *Memoirs of George III. 1845*

Weir, Alison: *Britain's Royal Families. Random House (Pimlico), 1996, Revised Edn.*

Printed in the United Kingdom
by Lightning Source UK Ltd.
9854800001B/55-72